SAUNDERS
PHYSICAL
ACTIVITIES
SERIES

Edited by

MARYHELEN VANNIER, Ed.D.
Professor and Director, Women's Division
Department of Health and Physical Education
Southern Methodist University

and

HOLLIS F. FAIT, Ph.D.
Professor of Physical Education
School of Physical Education
University of Connecticut

FOLK
DANCING

MILDRED C. SPIESMAN, Ed.D.

Associate Professor of Health and Physical Education
Queens College
Flushing, New York

ILLUSTRATED BY VERNON HÜPPI

W. B. SAUNDERS COMPANY
PHILADELPHIA • LONDON • TORONTO

W. B. Saunders Company: West Washington Square
Philadelphia, Pa. 19105

12 Dyott Street
London, WC1A 1DB

1835 Yonge Street
Toronto 7, Ontario

Saunders Physical Activities Series

Folk Dancing   SBN 0-7216-8518-8

Print No.   9   8   7   6   5   4   3   2

EDITORS' FOREWORD

Every period of history, as well as every society, has its own profile. Our own world of the last third of the twentieth century is no different. Whenever we step back to look at ourselves, we can see excellences and failings, strengths and weaknesses, that are peculiarly ours.

One of our strengths as a nation is that we are a sports-loving people. Today more persons — and not just young people — are playing, watching, listening to, and reading about sports and games. Those who enjoy themselves most are the men and women who actually *play* the game: the "doers."

You are reading this book now for either of two very good reasons. First, you want to learn — whether in a class or on your own — how to play a sport well, and you need clear, easy-to-follow instructions to develop the special skills involved. If you want to be a successful player, this book will be of much help to you.

Second, you may already have developed skill in this activity, but want to improve your performance through assessing your weaknesses and correcting your errors. You want to develop further the skills you have now and to learn and perfect additional ones. You realize that you will enjoy the activity even more if you know more about it.

In either case, this book can contribute greatly to your success. It offers "lessons" from a real professional: from an outstandingly successful coach, teacher, or performer. All the authors in the *Saunders Physical Activities Series* are experts and widely recognized in their specialized fields. Some have been members or coaches of teams of national prominence and Olympic fame.

This book, like the others in our Series, has been written to make it easy for you to help yourself to learn. The author and the editors want you to become more self-motivated and to gain a greater understanding of, appreciation for, and proficiency in the exciting world of *movement*. All the activities described in this Series — sports, games, dance, body conditioning, and weight and figure control activities — require skillful, efficient movement. That's what physical activity is all about. Each book contains descriptions and helpful tips about the nature, value, and purpose of an activity, about the purchase and care of equipment, and about the fundamentals of each movement skill involved. These books also tell you about common errors and how to avoid making them, about ways in which you can improve your performance, and about game rules and strategy, scoring, and special techniques. Above all, they should tell you how to get the most pleasure and benefit from the time you spend.

Our purpose is to make you a successful *participant* in this age of sports activities. If you are successful, you will participate often—and this will give you countless hours of creative and recreative fun. At the same time, you will become more physically fit.

"Physical fitness" is more than just a passing fad or a slogan. It is a condition of your body which determines how effectively you can perform your daily work and play and how well you can meet unexpected demands on your strength, your physical skills, and your endurance. How fit you are depends entirely on your participation in vigorous physical activity. Of course no one sports activity can provide the kind of total workout of the body required to achieve optimal fitness; but participation with vigor in any activity makes a significant contribution to this total. Consequently, the activity you will learn through reading this book can be extremely helpful to you in developing and maintaining physical fitness now and throughout the years to come.

These physiological benefits of physical activity are important beyond question. Still, the pure pleasure of participation in physical activity will probably provide your strongest motivation. The activities taught in this Series are *fun*, and they provide a most satisfying kind of recreation for your leisure hours. Also they offer you great personal satisfaction in achieving success in skillful performance —in the realization that you are able to control your body and its movement and to develop its power and beauty. Further, there can be a real sense of fulfillment in besting a skilled opponent or in exceeding a goal you have set for yourself. Even when you fall short of such triumphs, you can still find satisfaction in the effort you have made to meet a challenge. By participating in sports you can gain greater respect for yourself, for others, and for "the rules of the game." Your skills in leadership and fellowship will be sharpened and improved. Last, but hardly least, you will make new friends among others who enjoy sports activities, both as participants and as spectators.

We know you're going to enjoy this book. We hope that it—and the others in our Series—will make you a more skillful and more enthusiastic performer in all the activities you undertake.

Good luck!

MARYHELEN VANNIER

HOLLIS FAIT

CONTENTS

Chapter 6

Chapter 7

CHAPTER 1

HISTORY AND DEFINITIONS

Since the time of man's appearance on earth, he has danced. It is believed that, using the rhythmic quality inherent in his body, he first imitated the movements of animals and birds and then, long before speech was developed, discovered the value of repetitive rhythmic movement as a means of communication. Records of primitive man indicate that he danced to speak of the hunt and kill of an animal or an enemy and from this made an easy transition to talk with unseen gods, whom he felt controlled much of his destiny. With the passing of time, the primitive form of man's life gradually gave way to the ancient societies. From documents, paintings, and sculpture which have been found, it is known that dance held a fundamental place in the lives of the Israelites, the Egyptians, the Greeks, and the Romans. It was used in their cultures for religious worship, entertainment, the training of warriors, and as a means of giving outward form to beliefs, emotions, and events which made up their way of life.

Following the decline of the Roman Empire, western civilization moved into the period of the Dark Ages, during which the masses of people concentrated their attention on preparing for the life after death. There was no place in the monastic form of life for earthly pleasures and, as a result, dance almost passed out of existence. It was not until the excessive interest in religion started to diminish, during the Renaissance and the Reformation (1300-1576), that there was a revival of interest in the activity. During the first two centuries of its rebirth, dance was established and developed on the two levels on which it exists today. Ballet emerged as a performing art, and dancing as a recreational activity of the people came into being.

By the seventeenth and eighteenth centuries, social dancing had acquired widespread popularity in many parts of the western world. The aristocracy gathering at elaborate balls performed stately dances such as the Allemand, which befitted their social stature. They were also "trying their feet" on refined and complicated steps which

1

dancing masters frequently designed from the dance patterns of the peasant class. Meeting on the village square or in an open field, the dancers of the lower class moved in a wild and boisterous manner, gradually evolving set dances in conjunction with their everyday activities and experiences. Like their ancestors of earlier civilizations, they gave outward expression to their feelings and beliefs. "Speaking without words," as Plato described dance, they talked of their superstitions, occupations, and customs related to such important happenings as birth, courtship, marriage, and death. Passed down from generation to generation, these dances formed the foundation of today's folk dancing. Although the major portion of folk dances stems from the social dancing of the peasants, recognition and credit must be given to the dancing of the upper class. In many instances the modifications and changes in steps and patterns which they made are now the forms in which the movements are executed.

FOLK DANCING IN AMERICA

To many people, the words "folk" and "square" are synonymous when used in reference to the traditional dances of the United States. This is an error and may be caused in part by the nostalgic habit of Americans to remember the history of their country primarily in terms of the colorful pioneer days in the West. It cannot be denied that dancing in a square formation was extremely popular during the nineteenth century period of westward expansion. It should, however, be realized that it is only one of several types of American folk dancing. Line dances, circle dances, and play-party games also have contributed to the dance heritage of this country.

Almost all of the traditional dance materials of this country can be traced to two sources. The simple country dances brought by the early settlers from the British Isles and the relatively elaborate and intricately designed dances of the French. Brought to a land which neither physically nor culturally resembled the countries in which they originated, it is only natural that these European dances assumed new characteristics. Just as the people changed their customs and intermingled to become natives of their new society, so did their dances. Steps and dance figures originally executed with much posturing and exact posing were modified and performed in a much simpler manner. Too, national dances blended together, and the distinctive ethnic quality which they originally contained gradually gave way to a style that was typically American.

Square Dances

The four-sided formation of the square dance with its eight dancers is the most difficult of all American folk dances to trace to its original source. It is an established fact that the popular and well known "squares" which the pioneers took west in the early nineteenth century were American versions of the French quadrille. It is on the point of how the square formation first came to this country that there is considerable disagreement. Some authorities claim that seventeenth century French settlers brought it with them as a part of their cotillion dances. Other experts credit the square formation to the English and believe that it crossed the ocean in book form. In John Playford's very popular series, *The English Dancing Master— Plaine and Easy Rules for the Dancing of Country Dances, with the Tunes to Each Dance,* three dances are described which use the square formation. It is thought that one or more of the editions, which were published intermittently between 1651 and 1728, were brought to this country, and thus the four-sided formation was introduced and used. A third group of dance historians takes a middle position. They are of the opinion that settlers from the British Isles introduced the dance and document their belief with the eight couple square sometimes used in the Kentucky Running Set. However, they credit the contra dances of the French with limiting the number of couples to four and thus establishing the formation which is used in American square dancing.

The American square dance takes its characteristics and much of its terminology from the diverse people who danced it and who continue to dance it. Unlike European folk dances, which have retained almost the same basic patterns from generation to generation, square dancing keeps changing and reflecting the customs and attitudes of the day. Basically the dances performed today are the same as they were a century ago, but the manner in which they are danced and the calls which are given are totally different. Calling, one of the most outstanding characteristics of square dancing, is strictly an American invention. At one time, printed directions were sold to the dancers but this had many drawbacks. Far too many dances were being made up for written instructions to keep abreast of the changes, and many persons could neither read nor afford the items on which the directions appeared. Thus the caller came into existence with his colorful patter and singing calls. His ingenuity and skill in blending the figures of a dance together give square dancing its regional and local characteristics and prevent it from becoming a stereotyped form of folk dancing.

Line Dances

The roots of the square formations cannot be clearly traced, but there is no question as to the source from which the American line or longway set developed. Contra dances, as they most frequently are called, can be directly traced to one form of the English country dances. The word "contra" has been borrowed from the French "contredanse," which implies that couples stand opposite each other to perform the dance. However, the dance itself is a direct descendant of the English longway or line dance and retains two of its major characteristics: it is a dance in which an unlimited number of couples may participate in one set; and it has the distinctively English feature of longway dancing which is progression from head to foot couples.

During the seventeenth and eighteenth centuries, longway dancing was all the rage in England, and its popularity spread to the neighboring countries of Scotland and Ireland where it was danced almost as much as the native jigs and reels. It is not surprising that on immigration to America these people brought the dance with them. Many of the Scotch, Irish, and English settled in the northeastern section of the country, and it is with this region that the dance is associated. Living and working together, each of these national groups contributed to the development of the American form of contra dancing. All were well versed in the figures and steps of the numerous contras performed in their native countries (by the year 1728 there were over 900 in England alone) and with their inborn love for dancing found many occasions for gathering and performing them. With their highly developed technique and skill in executing dance steps, the English and Scotch probably made the greatest contribution to the new and combined figures and patterns that were to give the contra dances their American form. Through their efforts, the English "Sir Roger De Coverly" became the "Virginia Reel" just as the "Scottish Reform" was to change into the dance now called "Hull's Victory." The Irish settlers did not contribute extensively to the movements of the American contras, but much credit must be given to them for the gay and lilting music used for accompaniment. Such tunes as "Turkey in the Straw" and "The Girl I Left Behind Me" are but two of the many songs which they composed as part of the folk music of their adopted country.

Circle Dances

The enthusiasm of the New Englanders for contra dancing was not fully shared by the people who settled in the southern part of the country. Longway sets were included in the dancing of eighteenth century Virginia and other regions of the South but at no time did they challenge the circle dance or replace the affectionate feeling which the people had for them. The formation of dancing in a circle or ring can be traced back to paleolithic dances around tombs and ancient ritual dances with their motifs of consecration and protection. The manner in which circle dances were performed in the southern colonies, however, has its roots in English dances in which the dancers went "visiting." Couples or individuals progressing around the circle would dance with a new couple or an individual with each advance.

Circle mixers are enjoyed in all parts of the United States. In most regions they have acquired a characteristic formation of an even number of couples established in sets of four. In the South, this so-called American style is not always used. In developing their dances, the Southerners made numerous changes. In place of the double circle, which results from couples facing couples, they frequently used a single circle in which any number of couples, odd or even, may participate. In some of their favorite dances only one couple is active at any one time. On completing their visiting and dancing with all other couples in the circle, they are replaced by the second couple, and so on until all couples have "moved out" to dance. In other dances, couple one initiates the dance with couple two and moves on to couple three. When couple one is starting to dance with couple four, couple two advances to couple three. In a very short time, every couple in the circle is actively participating. The unique forms in which this "mixer" appears in the southern section of the country gives these circle dances a regional as well as a national style.

Play-Party Games

The play-party is a distinct form of group dancing which came into being in American communities where people were dependent upon their own resources for entertainment or in areas where dancing was looked upon as a symbol of sin. Rooted in the customs and traditions of the countries from which early settlers came, these so-called games have an ancestry of Scotch, English, Irish, and German songs and figures.

The attitude of various religious sects which settled in this country played an important part in the establishment and growth of play-party games during the pioneer days. The Methodists, Quakers, Baptists, and others differed in their form of worship, but they were in complete agreement concerning dancing. It was a wicked sport which one neither participated in nor watched. Strangely enough, there was full approval given to the traditional "playing games," which were a cross between dancing and the singing games of young children. Since they were not accompanied by a musical instrument (especially the fiddle which was considered a tool of the devil), they were acceptable.

Old-time play parties would begin at sundown and from miles around whole families would gather to enjoy the singing and rhythmic actions of such tunes as "Old Dan Tucker" and "Skip to My Lou." Actually the best of both dancing and singing games were retained in this crossbreed form. To the dramatic devices of the game, such as choosing or stealing a partner, were added certain dance figures and steps. The partner swing of square dancing was often used but with a hand hold substituted for the close, body contact position. The leader at a play party had two main functions to perform. To keep the dancers entertained, he served as a caller in the sense that he led the singing, and on occasion he would improvise a verse or two, so that the actions being taken could be varied.

DEFINITIONS

Over a period of years, the terms "national dance" and "folk dance" have come to mean the same thing from continuous usage. The incorrect and loose usage of these two expressions can and frequently does lead to misunderstanding. Rightfully, the words "national dance" should be used only when reference is being made to folk dances of a country which are widely accepted and danced in all regions. Enjoying widespread popularity in their native lands, the Hambo of Sweden and the Csardas of Hungary are two examples of dances that can be correctly classified as national. By comparison, the term "folk dance" is much broader in meaning. It is best defined as referring to all authentic, traditional dances, of specific groups of people, which reflect either national or regional characteristics. Evolved in a normal and unplanned manner from beliefs, feelings, and activities common to all mankind, they are dances which over a period of years may or may not have acquired extensive approval in the country of origin. Stemming from such sources as religious rites, birth, courtship, marriage, death, superstitions, and daily occupations, folk dance serves as a link between the past and the present. From the set, unchanged patterns and movements of many of the dances and even from variations inadvertently created in others during the process of transmission from generation to generation, contemporary man is provided with a means to better understand the way of life of the people who preceded him on earth.

CHAPTER 2

THE BENEFITS OF FOLK DANCE

Since the time of ancient civilizations, there has been a recognition of the benefits which an individual can derive from group dancing. For centuries, educators and philosophers such as Socrates, John Locke, and Francis Parker stressed its importance in helping to create a harmonious balance between body and mind that results in the healthy growth of the total personality. It was not, however, until the increasingly complex pattern of today's living caused concern about the present and future welfare of their fellowmen that the values of dancing were fully accepted. Alarmed at the growing number of people who physically and mentally are unable to cope with twentieth century living, physiologists, psychologists, and social scientists have repeatedly issued statements concerning the need for constructive use of leisure time. In published reports, they have strongly urged people of all ages to participate in activities which offset the physically detrimental effect of "push button" living and which serve as escape valves for mental tensions that build up in the pursuit of daily occupation.

From studies and surveys recently concluded comes valuable evidence of the personal benefits that can be obtained from folk dancing as a recreational activity. Continued over a period of time, folk dancing contains many factors considered essential in developing and maintaining a satisfactory level of physical and mental health. For purposes of discussion, the personal benefits that may be acquired are grouped under three major headings—physical, social, and psychological. It should be recognized that this division of man's personality into three separate areas is merely an administrative device. In actuality, it is impossible to assign specific benefits to any one area, since all parts of man's being constantly act and react with one another.

PHYSICAL BENEFITS

During the past decade, the term "physical fitness" has come into common usage, indicating a level of well-being that physiologists

7

believe everyone should maintain. It is a relative expression meaning different things to different people. In general, however, it implies a sufficiently high quality of organic vigor, muscular strength, co-ordination, flexibility, and agility to permit an individual to partici-pate in daily living without undue fatigue and to physically cope with unforeseen emergencies. When factors such as good nutrition, regular sleep, and avoidance of infections are included in the care of the body, it is known that a suitable level of physical fitness is best developed and retained through continuous participation in activities which are based on exercise.

When properly learned and practiced in good form, the rhythmic patterns and movements of folk dance provide an excellent means of exercising. Due to the wide variety of steps which are used and the varying degrees of speed of the music accompanying them, it is a form of exercise in which a wide age range can participate. For the young, it can be a vigorous activity. For members of the older genera-tion, it can be modified so that there are no detrimental physical or organic effects.

In addition to helping develop and maintain a level of fitness which results in more efficient and effective daily life, it is possible to derive the following physical benefits from continued folk dance participation:

1. Good posture and a coordinated, graceful body carriage.
2. The retention of body suppleness for a longer period of time.
3. The acquisition and refinement of motor skills to a level of proficiency which not only is self-satisfying but often results in recog-nition and approval by others.

SOCIAL BENEFITS

The continuous social interaction which occurs in folk dance provides innumerable opportunities for learning and practicing social amenities, as well as the building of better human relationships. Situations constantly arise when persons are dancing together in which the act and the consequences of the act are felt and seen almost immediately. Because of this, it is possible for an individual to quickly recognize and understand the importance of conducting himself in a manner which results in group approval. Social traits such as cour-tesy, respect and consideration for others, and cooperation cannot be acquired or developed through folk dance participation, however, if the person in charge of the activity is not aware of or concerned with these values. A social environment must be established and controlled if the skill of "getting along with people" is to be properly learned and practiced.

Other social benefits which may be derived from folk dance are:

1. The opportunity to make new friends.
2. A better understanding of and appreciation for the cultural heritage of ethnic groups.
3. The development of a wide variety of hobbies concerned with folk dance such as the history of specific dances, the symbolism of different costumes, and the music and native instruments used for accompaniment.

PSYCHOLOGICAL BENEFITS

Folk dance is a "fun" activity which takes place in a noncompetitive setting. It is primarily for this reason that the activity has much to contribute to the emotional well-being of the individual who participates. In a relaxing atmosphere, persons with a wide range of motor skill ability can attain a feeling of success and enjoyment. The hesitant and timid persons as well as those claiming "two left feet" are able to perform, without long hours of drill and practice, a number of dances which require simple steps. On the other hand, individuals with a well developed "sense of rhythm" can find pleasure and have a sense of accomplishment by participating in dances which use intricate and complicated patterns. In both instances, for the beginning as well as the advanced dancers, a basic need common to all mankind has been satisfied, which is to succeed.

Many of the psychological benefits that may be obtained through folk dance are closely related to benefits already assigned to the physical and social facets of man's personality. For example:

1. The development of steps and patterns to a well-coordinated and graceful level of movement can result in group recognition and approval, which, in turn, can dispel many emotional tensions created by a feeling of insecurity.
2. Interest in one or more of the many facets of folk dance as a hobby can serve as an "escape valve" for the emotional stresses which build up during daily living.
3. Learning and practicing social amenities can help develop a poised and confident manner of behavior.
4. Meeting people and making new friends can assist in breaking emotional barriers of excessive shyness and reserve.

SUMMARY

There are many factors inherent in folk dance which can be beneficial to the person who participates in the activity over a period of time. Since it offers a form of exercise which can be controlled to meet individual needs, it can help to develop and maintain a level of physical and organic fitness which results in a feeling of well being and more effectual daily living. Too, as a group activity which lacks the element of competition, it provides a setting in which social and emotional growth and development can take place. Since the personality of a human being is tightly interwoven, the physical and mental benefits derived from folk dance are constantly interacting; the contributions which the activity can make in one area often are of value in other areas.

CHAPTER 3

FUNDAMENTAL MATERIALS

To fully participate and enjoy folk dancing, the dancer must be familiar with the materials which serve as its foundation. In this chapter, many of the elements are presented. The most commonly used dance positions are described and illustrated and a number of dance formations appear in pictorial form. Salient points concerning leading and following are explained, since many folk dance figures are performed in social dance form. Because of the importance of correct form and the need for rhythmic understanding of steps and combinations of steps which are used in folk dancing, an analysis is made of fundamental dance movements and an easy-to-read reference chart of the rhythmic relationship of the movements to music is included. To provide an opportunity for practicing the material discussed in the chapter, a variety of popular folk dances of graduated difficulty are also analyzed.

DANCE POSITIONS

In almost all folk dances, the dance positions which are used by couples are merely variations of three basic types:

1. Side-by-side position with partners facing in the same direction, (Fig. 1); 2. Side-by-side position with partners facing in opposite directions, (Fig. 2); 3. Face-to-face position, (Fig. 3).

Side-by-Side Positions (Facing in Same Direction)

When standing alongside of each other and facing in the same direction, the girl is most frequently on the boy's right side. By the placement of hands and arms in different positions, a variety of dance positions can be created.

11

Figure 1. Side-by-Side Position, Partners Facing Same Direction

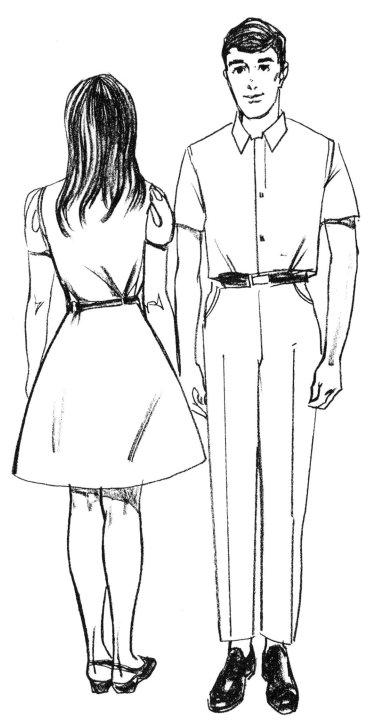

Figure 2. Side-by-Side Position, Partners Facing Opposite Direction

Figure 3.   Face-to-Face Position

Open position

The inside hips are touching; the boy's right arm is extended, brought across the small of the girl's back; and the hand is placed on the girl's waist at the right side. The girl's left hand rests lightly on her partner's right shoulder. The boy's left arm and the girl's right arm is dropped to the side of the body or placed in a posed position as designated for a specific dance.

Figure 4. Open Position

Open position with inside hands joined

The inside hips are touching; the boy's right and the girl's left hands are joined. Unless otherwise indicated, the elbows of the inside arms are bent and the joined hands are brought upward to approximately the height of the girl's shoulder. Free arms hang at the sides of the body.

Figure 5. Open Position with Inside Hands Joined

Semi-open position

The inside hips are in close proximity; the boy's right and the girl's left arm and hand are placed as explained in open position. Boy's left and girl's right arms are extended slightly forward and hands are joined.

Figure 6. Semi-Open Position

Promenade or skater's position

The inside hips are touching; the left hands are joined, with the boy bringing his left arm, elbow bent, across his body slightly below waist height. The right hands are joined and held in front of the girl. The boy's right arm is usually crossed on top of the girl's left arm.

Figure 7. Promenade Position

Back cross or backward skater's position

The inside hips are touching; the girl's left arm is extended across the small of the boy's back, and the left hands are joined on or near the left side of the boy's waist. The boy's right arm crosses on top of the girl's left arm and the right hands are joined and placed on or near the right side of the girl's waist.

Figure 8. Back Cross Position

Varsouvienne position

The girl stands at side and slightly forward on boy's right side. Left hands are joined with elbows bent and are brought up to approximately chest height on the boy's right side. The boy's right arm is extended across the girl's upper back but not touching her back. The girl's right elbow is bent and the forearm is raised so that right hands can be joined at approximately the height of the girl's shoulder but they do not touch the shoulder.

Figure 9. Varsouvienne Position

Butterfly of varsouvienne position

Frequently used in American square dancing as a promenade position or to perform dances using the varsouvienne pattern. This dance position is a variation of the position described above. The boy's right arm is slightly curved; the girl cuddles with the boy's arm resting lightly on her back. The joined right hands usually rest lightly on the girl's right shoulder.

Side-by-Side Positions (Facing in Opposite Direction)

When the couple stands alongside of each other, facing in opposite directions, the girl may be on either the right or left side. When two or more couples take a shoulder position, a single circle is formed with left shoulders facing center to move counterclockwise and with right shoulders facing center to move clockwise.

Elbow or hand swing position

With a close right to right (or left to left) hip position, the boy bends his right elbow (or left) and the girl slides her right (or left) arm through and contact is made on the inner part of both bent elbows. For a fast turn, partners pull slightly against the hooked arms which are tensed. The free arms usually are brought up to shoulder or head height and held in a graceful curved line. In a hand swing, a right to right (or left to left) hand grasp is taken with the four fingers wrapped around the partner's wrist. Arms are slightly bent at the elbow, and, on a fast turn, partners pull against each other with the arms and hands in complete tension (Fig. 10).

Buzz step or walking step swing position

To simplify getting onto this position, the couple starts in a closed dance position as described on page 27. Retaining the position of the arms and hands, the boy and girl move diagonally forward to the right (or left) side of their partner with hips touching. In moving into the position, the boy should slide his right hand from the small of the girl's back to the side of her waist. With the side position taken, the inside feet are kept close together to form a pivot point. In a buzz step swing, the outside feet are used continuously from a backward position. In a walking step swing, extremely small forward steps are used. Free hands usually are held at head height with arm in a graceful, curved line (Fig. 11).

Figure 10. Elbow or Hand Swing Position

Figure 11. Buzz Step Swing Position

Star or mill positions

This is usually performed by two or more couples in a single circle formation. In many dance descriptions the star or mill position is formed by extending the inside arms toward the center of the circle at approximately waist height and piling one hand on top of the other. In other descriptions, it requires that the inside arms be raised upward and extended inward with all hands touching. In American square dances, the position frequently is taken with inside arms, elbows slightly bent, extended toward the center of the circle, and each dancer grasping the wrist of the person in front of him.

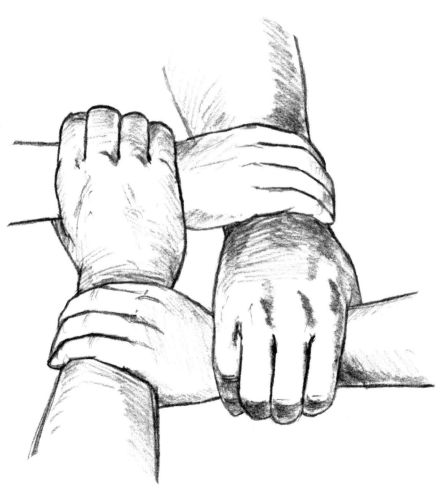

Figure 12. Star Position

Face-to-Face Positions

Two-hand hold position

Standing directly in front of each other, the partners join hands, a left with a right hand and a right with a left hand. Elbows are bent and the upper arms are kept in close to the body.

Figure 13. Two-Hand Hold Position

Shoulder-waist or polka position

The couple stand almost in front of each other, the girl very slightly to the boy's right; the boy places his two hands on the sides of the girl's waist with his elbows bent and his upper arms kept in close proximity to his body. The girl, bringing her arms forward with elbows slightly bent, places her hands lightly on her partner's shoulders.

Figure 14. Polka Position

Closed dance position

To perform waltz turns in a closed position, the girl stands facing her partner but somewhat to his right side, so that her right foot is in a position directly centered to his closed feet position. The boy places his right hand on the girl's back, somewhere between the lower part of her left shoulder blade and the small of her back. With the upper part of his left arm kept close to the body, the boy bends his elbow and brings the forearm upward almost to the height of his left shoulder. The girl's left arm, elbow slightly bent in a graceful curve, is brought forward and the hand rests lightly on the partner's right shoulder. Her right hand is brought forward and rests lightly in her partner's left hand. The position in which these hands are joined may vary slightly, but it is preferred that the girl place the four fingers of her hand between the boy's thumb and index finger and the boy gently wrap his fingers around the girl's hand.

Figure 15. Closed Dance Position

LEADING AND FOLLOWING

Folk dance patterns occurring in a set sequence or in positions other than the shoulder-waist or closed dance position do not need to be led, although it is frequently helpful to the girl if she is given an assist in making a turn or series of turns. However, when social dance patterns are required in a folk dance and partners must make a progressive pattern, it is extremely important that the boy understand and apply the principles of leading and that the girl recognize her responsibilities in following.

The old saying, "He who hesitates is lost," may very well have been written for the boy who is leading in a closed dance position or a shoulder-waist position. To lead effectively, he cannot stop or slow down to think. He must know where he is going and know exactly how he is going to get there with his partner. It is extremely

SINGLE CIRCLE	DOUBLE CIRCLE	LINE	OTHERS
No Partner	Partners Facing Counter Clockwise	File Line of 3	Square of 8 — Quadrille
Facing Center With Partner	Partners Facing	Lengthwise Set—Couples Facing Head	Triangle of 3
Partners Facing	Set of 2 Couples Facing	Longway Set — Couples Facing	Set of 2 Couples

Dance formations. The diagrammed formations are representative of the dances described in this book.

difficult, and many times impossible, for the boy to indicate properly the direction in which he wants the girl to move with him if he lacks the knowledge of where to place his feet and what to do with his body. An experienced dancer, after much practice, leads his partner almost unconsciously as he moves around a dance floor. The beginner, however, needs to first recognize the technique involved in leading and then concentrate on giving his partner the correct signals when he is practicing.

The boy assumes the major responsibility on a dance floor for the direction in which the couple moves, but it should be remembered that in the performance of any social dance patterns, in which counter-part movements are taken, it is a cooperative affair. The girl must assume certain obligations if the couple is to dance gracefully and with good style. In order to follow easily, she should:

1. Relax while she is dancing and continuously wait for her partner's lead.

2. Have her weight equally balanced on both feet in a pre-dance position and be prepared to move in any direction with either foot on receiving the correct lead.

3. Be sensitive to the lead being given by the boy's shoulders and from the release or increase of pressure which he applies with his right hand.

Pre-Dance Lead

When a folk dance starts with a social dance pattern, a definite lead should be given by the boy before he takes his first step. In a closed dance position, upward pressure is applied to the girl's back with the boy's right hand (with the hand slightly cupped, the pressure comes from the small finger side of the hand). In a shoulder-waist position, the upward pressure is applied from the cushions of the fingers of both hands. This pre-dance lead forces the girl to equally distribute her body weight on both feet and thus permits the boy to start dancing in the direction in which he wishes to move without having his partner anticipate the foot on which he will start.

Leading a Turn

To execute correctly any kind of turn (quarter, third, or half) it is necessary for the boy to use his shoulders and the upper part of his body. When turning to the left, starting from either a forward step left or a backward step off the right foot, the left shoulder is twisted backward and down as the upper body turns in the direction that the foot is pointing. In doing this, the right shoulder is forward and slightly upward. On turning to the right, the opposite is true.

Whether the turn starts forward right or backward on the left foot, the right shoulder twists backward and down and the left shoulder moves forward and slightly up. To make a turn, the foot must point in the direction in which the turn is to be made. The left foot stepping directly forward and toed out along with the shoulder movement will produce a turn to the left. The left foot stepping directly backward and toeing in (heel out) will create a turn to the right when the body is twisted in the direction that the foot is pointing. Using the right foot results in turns made directly opposite. Stepping forward on the right foot and toeing the foot out, twisting the shoulders to the right will create a right turn. Taking a step backward on the right foot, toeing the foot in, and turning the upper body in the direction that the foot points results in a left turn. If the foot and shoulders are moving correctly, they correspond. For a forward left turn starting with the left foot or for a backward left turn starting with the right foot, the foot is pointed to the left and the left shoulder is pulled backward and down. Turning right by starting with the right foot stepping forward or with the left foot stepping backward, the foot being used points to the right and the right shoulder is pulled backward and down.

At the time that the turn is being made, the boy must make sure that his partner remains in the position in which she started. To do this on a forward left turn, in closed dance position, he firmly but gently applies pressure to the girl's back with the heel of his right hand. On turning forward to the right in the closed position, he applies pressure with the cushions of the fingers of his right hand. In turning backward to the left or to the right, the application of pressure with the heel or the cushions of the fingers also is used along with simultaneous increased pressure in the right wrist and forearm to bring the girl in slightly closer to him. In a shoulder-waist position, it is much easier to keep the girl in the correct dance position. With a gentle but firm hold, with both hands on her waist, the boy will keep the girl directly in front of him.

FUNDAMENTAL MOVEMENTS AND COMBINATIONS

To be able to perform successfully the variety of patterns needed for specific folk dances, the dancer must be able to analyze rhythmically and perform correctly the movements and simple combinations on which they are structured. Classified as fundamental movements, they frequently appear in folk dances as the dominant pattern. When they are used in this manner, they should assume the style which is characteristic of the country in which the dance originated. For example, in many French dances, a series of running steps usu-

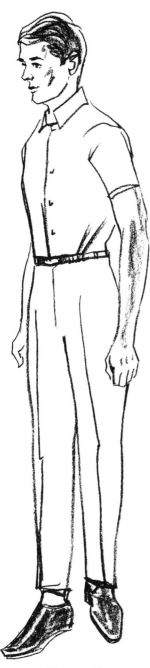

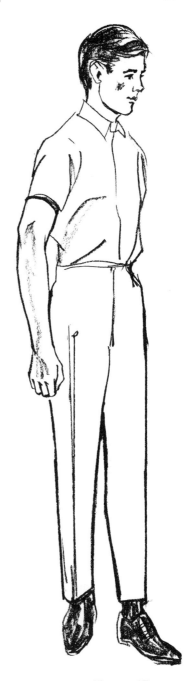

Figure 16   **Figure 17**

Body Turn Positions

ally have a light tripping quality. Performed in many German dances, these same steps would have a heavier quality, with emphasis placed on the accented beat of the music measure. Style is not discussed in the analysis of fundamental movements and combinations which follows, but it is important that the proper form be given to them when specific dances are learned.

Walk

For dance purposes, a walk is a series of steps taken in any direction and performed in an even rhythm. Each step is given the duration of one beat of music.

The length of a walking step in folk dances is dependent upon the tempo of the music, the accented beat, or on both tempo and accent. However, the structure of the movement does not change from its everyday use. Walking is initiated with a push off diagonally backward against the ground with the balls and toes of one foot. With the push off completed, the leg swings forward with flexion that starts at the hip joint. The knee and the ankle follow, sufficiently lifting the foot to clear the floor. The weight of the body is transferred from the heel of the foot to the ball and toes of the opposite foot as the next push off is taken. As a series of walking steps are taken, the feet point straight ahead and the inner borders of the feet are in parallel lines.

COMMON FAULTS

1. Walking with toes turned out or turned in.
2. Walking with feet too far apart or too close together.
3. Initiating the action of stepping from the knee or the foot.

Run

For dancing, the run should be called a fast walking step, since it does not have the body thrust or arm swing action usually associated with running. Performed in even rhythm, two running steps usually are given the duration of one beat of music.

To execute properly a series of running dance steps, the body leans slightly forward as a unit at the time the supporting foot contacts the floor. For a brief moment, there is no support as both feet leave the floor. On push-off and on landing, the body weight is first taken on the balls of the feet.

COMMON FAULTS

1. Landing with the body weight on heels with knees stiff.

2. Running with the body in an upright position.

3. Rotating legs outward or inward instead of bringing them forward and slightly upward.

Leap

In many respects, the coordination required to perform a leap is similar to that for a run. Frequently combined with walking or running steps taken in a forward or sideward direction, it is performed in an even rhythm with the action given the duration of one beat of music.

In a leap, the ankle and knee action are more pronounced than in a running step in order to achieve a longer period of supension. On pushing off with the ball of one foot, the knee of the free leg leads, and just prior to the moment when the foot starts to take the landing position, the leg is fully extended. The foot taking the push off is extended backward during the momentary suspension of the body.

COMMON FAULTS

1. Failing to push off with enough force to elevate the body.
2. Landing with body weight on heels, knees stiff.
3. Failing to extend the back leg during suspension of the body.

Jump

A jump carries the body upward and may take it slightly forward, backward, or sideward. Performed in an even rhythm, the jump usually is given the duration of one beat of music.

In executing a jump, the take off may be from one or both feet. After momentary suspension, the body drops back to the floor level with *the weight being taken on both feet.* The necessary height of the jump determines how much the knees are bent when the movement is initiated and how much the muscles of the legs should be tensed to push against the floor for the explosive upward action which is to be taken. On landing, the knees are bent and the body weight is first taken equally on the ball of the foot and then onto the full foot for balance.

COMMON FAULTS

1. Being off balance on the take off or landing by bending at waist and by failing to straighten legs and keep them hanging in line with body during suspension.

2. Bending knees and kicking heels upward following the take off.

3. Landing flat-footed with knees stiff.

Hop

A hop is a one-sided jump with the body being pushed into the air from one foot and, after a slight suspension, returning to floor level with *the weight on the same foot*. Taken as an isolated dance movement, the hop has an even rhythm and is given the duration of one beat of music. In combination with some patterns, such as the step-hop or schottische, it continues to receive the value of one beat. However, in combination with other patterns such as the polka, it may receive lesser value.

On pushing off from the floor, the same explosive power is needed as for a jump. During the moment of suspension, the knee of the free foot usually is slightly bent. At no time during the suspension or during the landing does this foot make contact with the floor. On landing on the same foot which initiated the action, the body weight is taken on the ball of the foot with the knee bent. The supporting leg is then straightened and the weight is placed on the full foot for balance.

COMMON FAULTS

1. Taking a leap instead of a hop.
2. Taking off on one foot and landing on the other.
3. Losing balance by bending at the waist.
4. Landing on the heel or flat of the foot with knee stiff.

Slide and gallop

Basically, the slide and the gallop are taken in the same form. The slide moves the body sideward, whereas the gallop produces a forward progression. Consisting of two movements, the slide and gallop are accompanied most often by music written in 2/4 and 6/8 meter. The advancing step in a sideward or forward direction with the quick closing action that follows receive the duration of one beat, with the first step being given the greater time value.

In the slide and gallop, the same foot is always in the advanced position and the step is taken on the toes and ball of the foot. The closing step which follows on the opposite foot is sharp and abrupt. This is caused by the pushing action that is used. As the two movements occur, the body weight is kept within the base of support for balance and for quick changes of direction. The action of quickly displacing the advancing foot with the closing step results in a slight lift off the floor and causes the pattern to be sometimes incorrectly analyzed as a step and hop.

COMMON FAULTS

1. Extending the body beyond the base of support and losing balance.
2. Failing to use an abrupt, sharp action to shift the body weight from the first to the second step.

Skip

Consisting of a walking step in combination with a hop, the skip is the most difficult uneven rhythm to perform. Associated with music frequently written in 4/4 or 6/8 meter, the two movements of the skip have the duration of one beat of music. The hop action has only one-half and sometimes only one-third the time value of the step. It is this uneven distribution of the beat which principally creates the problems which occur in learning to skip.

To skip, a step is taken forward or backward on one foot which is followed by a hop on the same foot. The knee of the free foot normally is bent and the foot is raised off the floor. On occasion, a stylized form of skipping is required, which necessitates that the free leg hang with the knee barely bent and kept in close to the supporting leg.

COMMON FAULTS

1. Failing to take the step and hop on the same foot. (Some persons are one sided "skippers" and will correctly perform the movements on one side but continuously substitute a leap for the hop on the next pattern.)
2. Leaning forward rather than lifting upward with the body on the hopping action.

Step-close

Two movements taken on an even rhythm with each movement often receiving the duration of one beat of music. Starting forward, backward, or sideward, the advancing foot takes a short step that is followed by the opposite foot moving into a position alongside of the supporting foot and taking the body weight.

1. Failing to take the body weight as the second step comes into the closed position.

Step arch

A two-movement combination frequently performed in folk dancing in conjunction with the waltz pattern. Usually taken sideward, a step is taken on the first beat, followed by a pulling of the free foot into closed position *without taking the body weight* on the second and third beats. In a few folk dances, this rhythm is reversed. The first step receives the first and second beats of the music measure and the arch pulls sharply into position on the count of three.

Common fault

1. Placing weight on the foot pulled into closing position.

Balance

There are many types of balance patterns. In square dancing, the balance consists of two movements. In the so-called folk dance balance, three movements are taken.

Used with music written in 2/4 meter, the square dance balance may be done in two different ways. With inside hands joined or with the boy's right hand holding his partner's left hand, couples face each other. Both may step backward with two steps (count 1, 2) and return to original position by stepping forward with two steps (count 1, 2), or they may take one step backward (count 1), point the free foot forward or swing it across the instep of the supporting leg (count 2), then step forward to original position and hold (count 1, 2).

The folk dance balance is most frequently performed to music written in 2/4 or 3/4 meters. Taken forward, backward, or sideward, the balance is developed from a step-close pattern with a change of weight in place.

2/4 Meter. Step left (count 1). Close right foot to left placing body weight on the ball of the foot with the heel slightly raised off the floor. (Count and) in place. Return body weight to left foot (count 2). Hold (count and).

3/4 Meter. Each movement as described above is given the time value of one beat. Step (count 1). Close (count 2). Change weight (count 3). The hold is omitted.

Common fault

1. Failing to change the body weight three times.

Two-step

A three-step combination taken to music written in 2/4 meter. Moving forward, backward, or sideward, the pattern is developed from a step-close and a walking step. The step-close equally share the time value of the first beat of the measure and the walking step is given the time value of the second beat.

COMMON FAULTS

1. Reversing the combination and starting with the walking step.
2. Failing to take the change of weight on the closing step.

FOLK DANCES

The following folk dances are organized on a graduated level ranging from simple to complex. They provide an opportunity for performing and practicing the fundamental movements discussed in this chapter. In describing the dances, credit has been given to the source from which the author first learned the dance.

Sicilian or Circassian Circle (United States)

Formation:	Sets of two facing in double circle. Girl on boy's right.
Music:	Folkraft 1140
Meter:	2/4
Source:	Folkraft Records outline
Pattern:	Walking steps.

MEASURES

Figure I Call: Forward and Back and Circle Four

1—4

Join inside hands with partner. Starting right, take 4 walking steps forward (counts 1—2, 1—2) and 4 steps backward to place (counts 1—2, 1—2).

5−8   All join hands and circle clockwise with 8 walking steps, finish in original positions.

Figure II Call: Ladies Chain

1−8   Two ladies change places with 4 steps, touch right hands in passing right to right shoulders. Join left to left hands with opposite man and with 4 steps make a courtesy turn. (See Glossary.) Repeat ladies chain, courtesy turn with partner, and finish in original positions.

Figure III Call: Right and Left

1−8   Moving forward to opposite side with 4 steps passing right to right shoulders. Standing side by side facing with partner make a half turn as a *couple* with four steps, finish facing opposite couple. Repeat action returning to original place.

Figure IV Call: Forward and Back, Forward and Pass

1−8   Repeat forward and backward action of measure 1−4, Figure I. Walk forward 8 steps, passing through opposites right to right shoulders and finish facing a new couple to repeat the dance.

Portland Fancy (United States)

Formation: Four people (2 couples) standing side by side, each lady on right of her partner, facing two other couples in a line. These sets of eight can be lined up the length of the room or a large quadruple circle can be established with the sets arranged like the spokes of a wheel.

Music: World of Fun M-104; Educational Dance Recordings FD-3; Folkraft 1131

Meter: 6/8

Source: Kirkell, Miriam H., and Schaffnit, Irma K. *Partners All—Places All!* New York, E. P. Dutton and Co., Inc., 1949, p. 28.

Pattern: Walking steps.

MEASURES

Figure I Call: Circle Eight Hands Around

1—8 Groups of eight join hands and circle once clockwise. Finish in original positions.

Figure II Call: Right and Left Through and Right and Left Back

9—12 All persons moving forward with 4 steps pass the opposite person right to right shoulders (right-left-right-left). Starting with lines back to back, each couple makes a courtesy turn (see Glossary) once and a half with 4 walking steps to finish facing opposite line.

13—16 Repeat measure 9—12 returning to original positions.

Figure III Call: Ladies Chain and Chain Right Back

17—20 All ladies 4 forward walking steps (right-left-right-left) toward opposite lady, touch right hands, and pass right to right shoulders. Join left hands with opposite man and with 4 steps make a courtesy turn.

21—24 Repeat action of measure 17—20 making courtesy turn with partner finishing in original position.

Figure IV Forward and Back, Forward Again and Pass Right Through

17—20 Lines of four join hands and walk

forward 4 steps and backward 4 steps (right-left-right-left).

21–24

All drop hands, walk forward 8 steps passing through opposites right to right shoulders to meet the oncoming set.

NOTE: If lines are set up the length of a room, when a line reaches the end of the room, they stand still for one repetition of the dance, turn around, and start dancing the other way when a line of four comes toward them.

When the dance has been repeated as many times as desired, the caller may say "Swing your partners and promenade." All swing partners and promenade counterclockwise.

Troika (Russia)

Formation:

Line of three. Boy in center, two girls on ends. Inside hands joined. Girls' outside hands on hips.

Music:

Folk Dancer M. H. 1059; Folkraft 1170; World of Fun M-105

Meter:

2/4

Source:

Neilson, N. P., Van Hagen, Winifred. *Physical Education for Elementary Schools.* New York, Ronald Press, 1954, p. 373.

Pattern:

Running steps, stamps.

MEASURES

Figure I Running Steps

1–4

Moving counterclockwise everyone starting on right foot, take 4 running steps diagonally forward right (counts 1 and 2 and). Take 4 running steps diagonally forward left (counts 1 and 2 and). Take 8 running steps directly forward (counts 1 and 2 and, 1 and 2 and).

Figure II Arch

5—6

In place. Boy and left-hand girl raise joined hands and form an arch. Right-hand girl goes under arch with 8 running steps starting right returning to place, while boy runs in place, follows her turning under his left arm. Left-hand girl runs in place facing counterclockwise. (Counts 1 and 2 and, 1 and 2 and).

7—8

Repeat measure 5—6 with left-hand girl going under arch formed by boy and right-hand girl. Boy follows her by turning in place under his right arm.

Figure III Circle

9—12

All join hands and circle clockwise with 12 running steps, starting right (counts 1 and 2 and, 1 and 2 and, 1 and 2 and). Stamp left-right-left. Hold (counts 1 and 2 and).

13—16

Repeat measure 9—12. Move counterclockwise starting on right foot.

Tropanka (Bulgaria)

Formation:

Single circle, without partners, facing center all hands joined at shoulder height, elbows bent.

Music:

Folk Dancer M. H. 1020

Meter:

2/4

Source:

Herman, Michael. *Folk Dances for All*. New York, Barnes and Noble, Inc., 1951, 2nd edition, p. 4.

Pattern:

Running step, step-hop, stamp.

MEASURES

Figure I   Running Steps and Stamps

1−2   Moving counterclockwise starting right, take 5 running steps (counts 1 and 2 and 1). Cross left foot front of right foot and stamp twice with no weight (counts and 2). Hold (counts and).

3−4   Repeat measure 1−2 clockwise starting left foot and stamping with right.

1−4   Repeat measure 1−4.

Figure II   Step-Hop Toward Center, Stamps and Back

5−6   Face center, take 2 step-hops (right-left) forward swinging free foot in front. Step sideward right, cross left foot over right foot and stamp twice and hold (counts 1 and 2 and).

7−8   Repeat measure 5−6 moving backward starting left. Stamp with right foot.

Figure III   Step-Hop Toward Center, Stamp and Shout "Hey"

5   2 step-hops (right-left) toward center of circle. Gradually bring hands over head and shout "Hey."

6   Step forward right (count 1). Stamp left foot twice in place (count and 2). Hold (count and).

7−8   Repeat measure 5−6 moving backward starting left, lowering hands to original position.

**Figure IV   Running Steps-
Stamps, Step-Hops**

9 — 12   Repeat measure 1 — 4 of Figure I.

13 — 16   Repeat measure 5 — 8 of Figure II.

Lech Lamidbar (Israel)

Formation: Single circle, no partners, facing
                                     center, hands joined downward.

Music: Israel Music Foundation LP 118;
                                     Folk Dancer M. H. 1093

Meter: 4/4

Source: Learned from members of a Hillel
                                     Foundation dance group.

Pattern: Step-hop, leap, grapevine.

MEASURES

Figure I

1   Moving   counterclockwise,   leap
                                     sideward, right (count 1), cross left
                                     foot in front of right (count 2), step
                                     sideward, right (count 3). Arch left
                                     to right (count 4).

2   Moving clockwise, step sideward,
                                     left (count 1), close right (count 2),
                                     step sideward, left (count 3). Arch
                                     right to left (count 4).

3 — 8   Repeat measure 1 — 2 three times.

Figure II

9   In place, step right (count 1). Hop
                                     right and swing left foot across in-
                                     step of right foot (count 2). Repeat
                                     step (count 3). Hop (count 4) with
                                     left foot, swing right foot.

10   Moving clockwise with grapevine
                                     pattern (see Glossary) starting with
                                     right foot crossing forward.

11—16	Repeat measure 9—10 three times.

Figure III

17—18	Step sideward right (count 1). Arch left to right and bend right knee (count 2). Repeat to left side (counts 3, 4). Step forward right, both knees bent and swing joined hands and arms forward and up (count 1). Step backward left (count 2). Arch right to left and hold (counts 3, 4).
19—20	Repeat measure 17—18.

Figure IV

21—22	Moving clockwise, 1 grapevine step starting with right foot (counts 1, 2, 3, 4). Cross right in front of left (count 1). Step sideward left (count 2). Jump (count 3). Hop onto right with left foot raised off floor, knee slightly bent (count 4).
23—24	Moving counterclockwise reverse the direction of measure 21—22 crossing left foot in front of right. End with hop left and right foot raised.
25—28	Repeat measure 21—24.

Kalamatianos (Greece)

Formation:	Open circle, elbows bent and close to body, hands joined at shoulder height and slightly forward of shoulders. Leader at right end of line carries a handkerchief which he twirls to indicate improvisations and changes in pattern. The men, especially the leader, dance in a majestic and dignified manner. The women frequently dance with their eyes downcast in a modest form. The movements which are taken

have a quality of controlled power and strength and are executed mostly on the flat of the foot.

Music: Festival   F3505B   "Samiotisa"; Olympic   OL24-13   "Picnic   in Greece"

Meter: 7/8. This meter for the dance pattern is broken into a Slow (counts 1, 2, 3). Quick (counts 4, 5). Quick (counts 6, 7) rhythm.

Source: The three "basic steps" described have been learned from Greek teachers and students of Greek folk dance.

Pattern: Walking steps, stamps.

MEASURES

Figure I   Facing Center

1   Step sideward right with right foot (slow) (counts 1, 2, 3). Step left in back of right (quick) (counts 4, 5). Step sideward right (count 6). Hop right (count 7) and turn almost into a file formation behind leader.

2—3   Moving on a slight diagonal forward with 3 steps (left-right-left) (slow-quick-quick). Step forward right (slow). Step forward left (quick). Close right to left (quick).

4   Step diagonally backward left-right (slow-quick). Close left to right turning to face center (quick).

Figure II   Approximate File Formation Following Leader

1—2   Step forward 3 steps (slow-quick-quick) starting right. Repeat starting left.

3—4

Softly stamp right foot. Step right and face center (slow). Step left crossing in front of right and lift right foot slightly off floor (quick). Step right in place and raise left slightly off floor (quick). Repeat measure 3 beginning with soft stamp on left facing center.

Figure III   Facing Center

1

Step sideward right (slow). Cross left back of right (quick). Step sideward right (quick).

2

Cross left in front of right (slow). Step sideward right (quick). Cross left in back of right (quick).

3—4

Step sideward right (slow). Cross left in front of right, lift right foot slightly off floor (quick). Step right in place, lift left foot slightly off floor (quick). Repeat measure 3 starting sideward left with left foot.

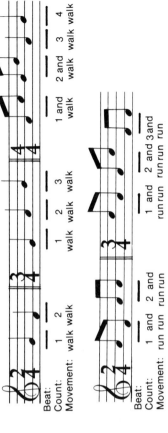

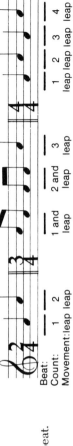

Walk

Taken in a series, each step is given the time value of one beat.

Run

Two running steps, usually given the time value of one beat.

Leap

Each leap given the time value of one beat.

Jump

Each jump given the time value of one beat.

Hop

When taken alone or in such combinations as a step-hop given the time value of one beat.

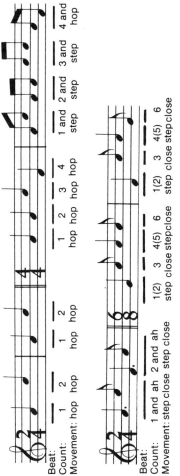

Beat:									
Count:	1	2	1	2	3	4	1 and	2 and	3 and	4 and
Movement:	hop	hop	hop	hop	hop	hop	step	step	step	hop

Slide and Gallop

The two movements are given the time value of one beat with the first movement receiving the greater value.

Beat:						
Count:	1 and ah	2 and ah	1(2)	3	4(5)	6
Movement:	step close	step close	step	close	step	close

Skip

The two movements are given the time value of one beat with the second movement (hop), receiving one-half or one-third of the time value given to the step.

Beat:						
Count:	1 and ah 2 and ah 3 and ah	4 and ah	1(2)	3	4(5)	6
Movement:	step-hop step-hop step-hop	step-hop	step	hop	step	hop

Step-Close

The two movements receive equal counts. In some patterns they equally share the time value of one beat as in the two-step. In 3/4 meter patterns each movement is given the time value of one beat.

Beat:					
Count:	1 and	2 and	1 and	2 and	1	2	3	1	2	3
Movement:	step-close step-close	step-close step	step close step close hop	step step close step close hop

(waltz)   (mazurka)

Balance

Three movement pattern. In 2/4 meter, the first and second steps equally share the time value of one beat. The third movement followed by a hold receives the time value of one beat. In music written in 3/4 meter, each movement receives the time value of one beat.

Beat:				
Count:	1 and	2 and	1	2	3
Movement:	step-close shift wt.-hold	step close shift wt.

CHAPTER 4

THE SCHOTTISCHE

BACKGROUND

Factual information about the dance called Schottische is vague and ambiguous. Some authorities believe that it is Scotch in origin and developed from the running steps and hops that were used in some of the early Scottish dances. Other experts, basing their opinion primarily on the name, claim that it was first danced in the German-Austrian area of Europe. And there are those who maintain that it is of "immemorial antiquity" and its roots are lost in the unwritten history of ancient civilization.

Even though it is difficult to trace its beginning, there is a wealth of information available which describes the popularity which it enjoyed during the 1800's as a ballroom dance. Nils Bergquist, noted Swedish dance leader, reports that a figure dance appeared in his country in the early years of this century and was a favorite of many people. Anatole Chujoy, in his *Dance Encyclopedia*, states that this dance was a popular stage, as well as social, dance in England and other European countries during the 1840's and 1850's. Fox and Merrill write that during the same period, it was being enjoyed in many parts of Poland. American historians of the nineteenth century make numerous references to the Schottische and the important place which it held in the fashionable salons and ballrooms of the large cities.

After many years of being one of the "must" dances at balls and social gatherings, the dancing public began to lose interest in the Schottische. It continued to be a part of folk dancing but under its proper name was seldom performed as a social dance. During the twentieth century, it reappeared as the basic step of the jitterbug and as a pattern of the Big Apple but the day of the Schottische with its well-executed movements has disappeared from the ballroom floor.

RHYTHMIC COUNT AND STYLE

The movements contained in the Schottische pattern appear in two forms and with two styles. The progression of step-close-step-hop

49

is referred to as the traditional pattern. The run-run-run-hop sequence has been given several names. It most frequently is called the modern Schottische but on occasion it is jokingly referred to as the barnyard step. This name probably is due to the brief revival of the pattern in this country about 1905. Performed as an old-time ballroom dance, it was called the Barn Dance.

Whether the traditional or modern version of the Schottische is used, the accompanying music can be written in either 2/4 or 4/4 meter. When performed to either meter, each movement is given the time value of one beat.

In performing the first three movements of the pattern whether step-close-step or a run-run-run sequence is used, they are taken smoothly with the first step slightly more pronounced than the other two in order to accent the first beat of the music measure. It is on the hop that the distinctive styles of the two forms of Schottische are most apparent. In the traditional pattern when the hop is taken, the free foot with the knee slightly bent barely lifts off the floor. The free foot is kept directly under the body and placed close to the ankle of the supporting leg. In the modern version, the hop is taken with a swing of the free foot. In some folk dances, the free foot is lifted slightly off the floor in a forward position. In others, the swinging motion is completed with the toes touching the floor or with the free foot being moved diagonally in front of the ankle of the supporting leg with the foot clearing the floor.

Many folk dance descriptions stipulate that the Schottische pattern be taken in a forward direction—directly forward, or on a forward diagonal. It is possible, though, for it to be included in a dance with movement in a backward or sideward direction. When the movement is in a sideward direction, the second step is frequently changed to a slight crossing step in back so that the pattern can be more easily performed. In moving backward it is a mistaken idea that on the hop, the free foot swings in the direction that the steps have been taken. For good style, the swinging movement should be taken in a forward direction.

SUGGESTED LEARNING PROCEDURE

The learning of the Schottische pattern may be undertaken in two ways. Experienced dancers and persons well trained in fundamental movements can and should learn the total pattern and quickly relate it to music and to dances in which it appears. For the inexperienced dancer, it may be necessary to break down the pattern and, through rhythmic verbalization of the action being taken and by counting the measure beats, gradually rebuild it. Approaching the Schottische pattern through the two-step pattern results in learning the traditional form. When a running step approach is used, the modern version of the pattern emerges.

Approach from the two-step pattern

1. Listen to music written for the Schottische which is being played at moderate speed in 4/4 meter. Clap the measure beats and verbalize the actions of the two-step pattern

Hands:	Clap	Clap	Clap	Clap
Pattern:	Step	Close	Step	Hold
Count:	1	2	3	4

2. Continue rhythmically to verbalize the actions and move in a forward direction starting the pattern on the left foot and repeating it to the right.

It may be necessary to learn the hop that occurs on the fourth beat of the Schottische pattern separately. Inexperienced dancers frequently confuse the hopping movement with the neuro-muscular coordination used for a leap. If it is necessary to isolate the hop, the action is more easily learned in connection with a step. STEP-HOP. Verbalize the two movements and practice, continuously remembering that the step and the hop are taken on the same foot. Some persons find this coordination extremely difficult and repeatedly throw their body weight on to the free foot (a leap) instead of keeping it on the same foot. If this keeps happening start skipping and gradually slow it down until the two parts of a skip, a step and a hop, emerge. Keep doing a very slow skip until the coordination can be both seen and felt.

3. With the coordination of a step and a hop acquired, the third and fourth movements of the schottische pattern have been mastered. First, with rhythmic verbalization and then as quickly as possible with music, move in a forward direction with the schottische pattern.

4. With music, practice the schottische step with a partner in an open dance position with inside hands joined. Both start forward on their outside foot.

Having learned the traditional style of the schottische pattern, use the same procedure to obtain the rhythmic coordination needed for the modern form. Substitute three running steps for the two-step pattern and quickly review steps 1 through 4. When practicing the modern schottische step with a partner, explore different ways in which it can be used.

FOLK DANCES

The following folk dances are organized on a graduated level ranging from simple to complex. They provide an opportunity for performing and practicing the Schottische pattern discussed in this chapter. In describing the dances, credit has been given to the source from which the author first learned the dance.

Road to the Isles (Scotland)

Formation:	Double circle of couples facing counterclockwise in Varsouvienne position.
Music:	Imperial 1005, Folk Dancer M. H. 3003, Educational Dance Recordings FD-2
Meter:	2/4
Source:	Wakefield, Eleanor Ely. *Folk Dancing in America.* New York, J. Lowell Pratt and Co., 1966, p. 115.
Pattern:	Point, grapevine, schottische.

MEASURES

Figure I   Point and Grapevine

1–3	Both partners point left foot forward (counts 1–2). Step left foot back of right (count 1). Step sideward right (count 2). Cross left in front of right and hold (counts 1–2).
4–6	Repeat action of measure 1–3 starting with right foot and moving sideward to left.
7–8	Point left foot forward and lean slightly back (counts 1–2). Point left foot backward and lean slightly forward (counts 1–2).

Figure II   Schottische Steps

9–12	Moving counterclockwise starting

with left foot take 2 forward schottische steps. On last hop, retaining hand hold positions, make a half-turn independently to the right to face clockwise. Girl in Varsouvienne position on boy's left side (counts 1−2, 1−2, 1−2, 1−2).

13−14   Moving clockwise starting with left foot take 1 forward schottische step. On the hop, retaining hand hold position, make a half-turn independently to left to face counterclockwise in original position (counts 1−2, 1−2).

15−16   Walk forward 3 steps (right-left-right) and hold (counts 1−2, 1−2).

NOTE: In some regions of this country, Figure I and Figure II are taken twice.

Ersko Kolo (Yugoslavia)

Formation: Single circle facing center, no partners, hands joined and held downward.

Music: Folk Dancer M. H. 3020

Meter: 2/4

Source: Krause, Richard, *Folk Dancing.* New York, The Macmillan Co., 1962, p. 85.

Pattern: Step-cross, schottische.

MEASURES

Figure I   Step-Cross

1−7   Moving counterclockwise slowly step sideward right with weight on heel (count 1). Cross left foot back

	of right (count 2). Repeat the step and cross action seven times.
8	In place, stamp right putting weight on foot (counts 1 and). Stamp left lifting foot slightly without weight (counts 2 and).
1−8	Moving clockwise repeat action of measure 1−8 starting sideward left. On last stamp (right) turn and face counterclockwise.

Figure II Schottische

9−16	Moving counterclockwise, starting on right foot, 1 schottische step forward (counts 1−2, 1−2). Moving clockwise 1 schottische step backward (counts 1−2, 1−2).
	Facing center of circle, 1 schottische step forward, starting right. Moving backward, 1 schottische step to re-form circle.
9−16	Repeat measure 9−16.

Rheinlaender for Three (Germany)

Formation:	Line of three facing counterclockwise. Man between two ladies. Inside hands joined and ladies outside hands on hips.
Music:	Folk Dancer M. H. 1050, Folk Dancer LD-12
Meter:	4/4
Source:	Harris, Jane A., Pittman, Anne, and Waller, Marlys S. *Dançe A While*. Minneapolis, Minnesota, Burgess Publishing Co., 1964, 3rd edition, p. 221.
Pattern:	Schottische, running steps.

MEASURES

Figure I Arches

1—2

Moving counterclockwise, starting with left foot, take 1 schottische step diagonally forward left (counts 1—2—3—4) and 1 schottische step diagonally forward right (counts 1—2—3—4).

3—4

Starting on the left foot, with 2 forward schottische steps, the lady on the right moves under arch formed by man and lady on the left. At the same time, the lady on the left moves to opposite position and man turns in place under his left arm. Finish facing clockwise.

5—8

Repeat action of measure 1—4 starting clockwise and finish facing counterclockwise.

1—8

Repeat action of measure 1—8.

Figure II Running Steps and Turn

9

Moving counterclockwise, starting on left foot, 4 forward running steps (counts 1—2—3—4).

10

Inside hands raised to form arches, both ladies make one complete turn under arms with 4 running steps (toward the man) while man takes 4 steps in place.

11—12

Moving backward repeat action of measure 9—10. Ladies turn away (outward) from man.

13—16

Repeat action of measure 9—12.

Fado Blanquita (Portugal-Brazil)

Formation:

Single circle of partners facing center. Hands joined with arms extended. Girl on boy's right.

Music: RCA Victor LPM 1620, Educational Dance Recordings FD-4

Meter: 4/4

Source: Originally learned at New York City Public School Workshop. Described by Festival dancers at Queens College.

Pattern: Walking steps, step-hop, schottische, jump and turn.

MEASURES

Figure I   Walking Steps

1—4   Moving counterclockwise 16 small walking steps starting on right foot. Turn body to step forward. On last step, turn body to face clockwise.

1—4   Repeat action of measure 1—4 moving clockwise. Finish facing center of circle.

Vamp

2 measures   Step sideward right (counts 1—2). Step sideward left (counts 3—4). Repeat right and left. Sway body slightly in direction of sideward step.

Figure II   Schottische Circling

5—7   Facing partner join right hands. With 3 forward schottische steps (boy starting left, girl starting right) make a complete circle finishing in original position.

8—10   Boy moving counterclockwise, girl moving clockwise, drop right hands and pass partner right to right shoulders with 1 forward schottische step. Join left hands with oncoming person and make a half-circle with 1 forward schottische step. (Girls are facing counterclockwise, boys are facing clockwise.) Drop left hands, pass left to left shoulders and rejoin right hands with partner. Make a half-circle with 1 forward schottische step finishing in original positions.

NOTE: Throughout this figure, the joined hands and arms should be fully extended.

11 — 16   Repeat action of measure 5 — 10.

Vamp

2 measures   Repeat Vamp as described facing center of circle.

Figure III   Jump, Turn, Walking Steps

17 — 18   In place, jump to stride position (feet about 12 inches apart) (count 1). Hold (count 2). Jump crossing right foot over left (count 3). Hold (count 4). Drop hands and slowly pivot right to face outward. Finish with backs to center of circle, feet parallel (counts 1 — 2 — 3 — 4).

19 — 20   Rejoin hands and repeat action of measure 17 — 18. Finish facing center of circle with hands joined.

21 — 24   Move forward toward center of circle with 4 slow walking steps (right-left-right-left) (counts 1 — 2 — 3 — 4, 1 — 2 — 3 — 4). Move backward to place with 4 slow walking steps.

25 — 32   Repeat action of measure 17 — 24.

Moskrosser (Denmark)

Formation: Sets of twos facing in double circle. Couple 1 facing clockwise. Couple

2 facing counterclockwise. Girl on boy's right.

Music and Source: RCA Victor EPA 4136

Meter: 4/4

Pattern: Schottische, step-hop.

MEASURES

Figure I   Schottische Forward and Backward

1–2   Couple 1 join inside hands and move forward in between couple 2 with 2 schottische steps. At the same time, couple 2 moves forward with 2 schottische steps on outside of couple 1. Boys start with left foot, girls with right foot.

3–4   Moving backward to place, couple 1 drops hands and takes 2 schottische steps going to the outside of couple 2. At the same time, couple 2 joins inside hands and takes 2 schottische steps going in between couple 1.

Figure II   Ladies Chain and Courtesy Turn

5–8   Ladies move forward, starting right foot, touch right hands, and passing right to right shoulders to opposite side with 2 schottische steps. Left to left hands joined with opposite man and make a courtesy turn (see Glossary) with 2 schottische steps.

9–12   Repeat action of measure 5–8 making courtesy turn with partner and finish in original position.

Figure III   Right Hand and Left Hand Stars

1–8   All four dancers extend right arms toward center and hands are piled. Facing clockwise, move forward, circling with 4 schottische steps starting on right foot. Drop hands, making a half turn inward, extend left arms and form a left hand star. Move forward, circling with 4 schottische steps. Finish in original positions.

Figure IV   Balance and Progress

9—10

Partners face, join inside hands (boy's right, girl's left). Take 1 small schottische step backward (boy starts with left foot, girl with right foot), 1 schottische step forward toward partner.

11—12

Couples take a shoulder-waist position. Turning clockwise while progressing counterclockwise around opposite couple take 4 step-hops to change places. Boy starts with left foot, girl starts right. Immediately face the oncoming couple with whom the dance will be repeated.

NOTE: As couples change places to form new sets, couple 1 continually move clockwise and couple 2 move counterclockwise.

Weggis Dance (Switzerland)

Formation:

Couples in double circle facing counterclockwise. Skaters position with right hands joined above left.

Music:

Folkraft 1170; Imperial 1008; World of Fun M101; Folk Dancer M. H. 1046

Meter:

2/4

Source:

Fox, Grace I., and Merrill, Kathleen G. *Folk Dancing.* New York: The Ronald Press Co., 2nd edition, 1957, pp. 67-69.

Pattern:

Heel-toe, polka, schottische (traditional form), step-hop, step-point.

MEASURES

Figure I Heel-Toe and Polka Forward

1

In place, with weight on right leg (both boy and girl start on the same foot). Extend left leg forward with heel touching floor (count 1). Touch left toe in front of right foot (count 2).

2

Moving counterclockwise with 1 polka step starting with hop on right foot.

3—4

Repeat action of measure 1—2 using right foot.

5—8

Repeat action of measure 1—4.

Chorus   Sideward Schottische Away and Back and Turn

9—10

Starting boy's left foot, girl's right foot take 1 schottische step away from partner and 1 schottische step toward partner.

11—12

Shoulder-waist position, take 4 step-hop patterns making one complete circle clockwise.

13—16

Repeat action of measure 9—12.

Interlude (2 measures)
During these two measures dancers take position for the next figure.

Partners face in single circle, boys facing counterclockwise and girls facing clockwise. Hand on outside held overhead in a curved graceful line. Inside arms held about hip high.

Figure II   Heel-Toe and Polka Inward and Out

1—8

Repeat action of measure 1—8 of

	Figure I. Boy starting on left foot and girl on right foot. Move sideward toward center of circle and then outward reversing arm positions.
9—16	Repeat Chorus of Figure I.
	Interlude (2 measures)
	Skaters position facing counter-clockwise with right hands joined on top of left hands.
	Figure III Step-Point and Polka Forward
1	Both partners step sideward left (count 1) and point right toe across left foot (count 2).
2	Repeat action of measure 1 stepping sideward right.
3—4	2 polka steps forward starting with hop on right foot.
5—8	Repeat action of measure 1—4.
9—16	Repeat Chorus of Figure I.
	Interlude (2 measures)
	Double circle, partners facing. Join right hands, elbows bent and forearms touching. Free hands on own hip.
	Figure IV Step-Point and Change Places
1—4	Repeat action of measure 1—4 of Figure III changing places with partner on the 2 polka patterns.
5—8	Repeat action of measure 5—8 of Figure III returning to original position on 2 polka patterns.
9—16	Repeat Chorus of Figure I.

Interlude (2 measures)

Double circle, partners facing. Boy's right hand joined with girl's left hand and arms extended at shoulder height. Free hands on own hips.

Figure V Step-Hop, Turns, and Bow

1   Drop joined hands, and boy, starting on left foot, girl starting on right foot, individually make one complete turn with 2 step-hops. Partners turn away from each other (count 1 and 2 and).

2   Join boy's left hand to girl's right hand, moving clockwise, step sideward (boy's left foot, girl's right foot), bring feet together, bow and curtsy.

3—4   Repeat action of measure 1—2 moving in opposite direction starting turn with boy's right foot, girl's left foot.

5—8   Repeat action of measure 1—4.

9—16   Repeat Chorus of Figure I.

CHAPTER 5

THE MAZURKA AND VARSOUVIENNE

BACKGROUND

The mazurka pattern used today in folk dances bears little resemblance to the sixteenth century Polish Mazur which is believed to be its parent dance. Almost all factual information about the Mazur identified with the Mazur people, living on the plains of Masowaze, has been lost in history. Authorities, however, are quite sure that originally it was a three-part dance. The Mazur or Mazurek, the Obertas or Oberek, and the Kujawiak, which came from the neighboring area of Kujawy, probably evolved from folk songs. More than 100 figures were used in the performance of the three portions of the dance but the manner in which they were combined apparently was left almost entirely to the inventiveness of the dancers. Only two movements have been found that continuously were used in the same form. They are stamping steps and heel clicking actions performed by the men in a set sequence.

The vigorous and sometimes wild dance which the Mazurs accompanied with song and dudy (a type of bagpipe) spread rapidly throughout Poland during the seventeenth century. On leaving its native land and traveling into Russia and then to other neighboring countries, the Mazur lost its name and acquired a more refined form. Calling it the Mazurka, the dancing masters for the aristocracy of European capitals continually changed many patterns and kept adding new ones. With the exception of a few simple figures, none of the revised or new steps ever became an established part of the dance. Writing about the dance in 1847, Henri Cellarius, the foremost of dance masters, called it an independent and truly inspiring dance which had no set format. Most of the patterns were left to the inventiveness of the dancers and most likely it was their lack of ingenuity which caused the dance to lose favor.

The Mazurka gradually disappeared from ballrooms and fashionable salons of the nineteenth century. Yet an offshoot of the dance continued to be popular. The Varsouvienne, which in the 1880's became known as the Varsovianna and a decade later was called Varsouvianna, may very well have originated in Poland in the 1850's. This may not be its source since some authorities credit it to figures found in a sketch book belonging to Cellarius. And there are still others who timidly suggest that the last half of the name suggests Vienna or perhaps it was named in honor of the Italian volcano, Mount Vesuvius. All of these varied ideas, right or wrong, concerning its place of origin can lead to only one conclusion. The Varsouvienne was widely danced throughout Europe in the last half of the nineteenth century and on traveling across the sea became one of America's favorite dances.

RHYTHMIC COUNT AND STYLE

The music accompanying the Mazurka and the Varsouvienne is written in either 3/4 or 3/8 meter. In performing the Mazurka, emphasis may be placed on either the second or third beat, since both contain heavily accented movements. When the pattern starts on the first beat of the music measure with a step, the closing or "cut" step occurring on the second beat is usually stressed. In starting with a swinging or sweep of the free foot with a hop on the supporting leg, an upbeat is needed and thereafter the last beat of each measure most often is accented. For the Varsouvienne, emphasis is placed on the third beat.

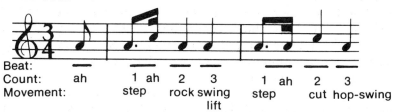

Beat:		—		—	—		—	—	—
Count:	ah		1 ah	2	3	1 ah	2	3	
Movement:		step		rock swing		step	cut hop-swing		
				lift					

The manner in which the mazurka pattern is executed and the style that is used differ extensively throughout the world. On the Island of Martinique in the West Indies, the original Mazurka imported by French colonists became mixed with the native Beguine resulting in a rocking pattern in place with a slight lift. Even though a heavy movement is taken on the first step, the Martinique Mazurka has a smooth and flowing quality. In Germany, the pattern, in some dances, consists of strong, vigorous movements whereas in others it takes on the dignity of a Waltz. In different countries as well as in many sections of one country, the Mazurka has assumed a style characteristic of the people, as is true of the Varsouvienne as it is danced in this country. Preferably called the Varsouvianna, the people of the southwest, especially New Mexico, perform the pattern with great energy and at a relatively fast speed. In other sections of the country, particulary in the east, the same movements are executed much more smoothly and at a slower pace.

SUGGESTED LEARNING PROCEDURES

The mazurka pattern may be learned through several approaches. To acquire the style and movements needed to perform the Martinique Mazurka, the rocking step approach is recommended. To obtain the sequence of movements necessary for the Varsouvienne and the Mazurka using the hop, it is suggested that the step-close approach be followed.

Approach from rocking steps

1. Listen to mazurka music (recommended record—Folkways FP840) and clap the underlying beats of each measure emphasizing the second beat.

2. Verbalizing the count and speed of the music, rock forward on the right foot on the count of one. Take a short step, bend the knee, and lean the body slightly forward. Let the left leg come slightly off the floor. On the count of two, rock the body weight backward on the left foot coming to an upright position. Raise the right foot slightly off the floor with the knee bent. On the count of three remaining in an upright position, swing the right freely over and slightly above the instep of the supporting leg almost touching the shinbone of the left leg with the right heel. Extend the right ankle and point the toes toward the floor.

Pattern:	Step forward	Rock backward	Swing
Feet:	R	L	R
Count:	1	2	3

3. Repeat these movements with verbal count until they can be performed in a graceful and flowing manner. Recognize that the same foot starts each pattern. Practice with the music starting on the right foot and then on the left foot.

4. To acquire the style of the Martinique Mazurka give the forward rocking step a heavy quality as the foot moves forward into place by bending the body slightly at the waist. On the third movement, as the free foot sweeps across the supporting leg, take a slight lifting action (no hop) by taking the heel of the supporting foot slightly off the floor.

Approach from a step-close

1. Listen to music arranged for the Mazurka that is written in 3/4 meter. Recognize the upbeat at the onset of the music and then clap the measure beats emphasizing the third. Continue to listen and clap, take two steps in place on the counts of 1, 2, and hold the third beat. Repeat this several times, recognizing that the pattern begins each time on the same foot. Practice the movements on the opposite foot.

2. With music and verbalizing the count, in place add a hop on the third beat. Step-step-hop.

3. First verbalizing and then with music, move on the count of 1, taking a gliding step forward (as though ice skating) on the right foot (knee is slightly bent and the body is leaning forward just a little as the foot slides forward). When the forward step is taken (right) extend the back leg (left) keeping the knee slightly bent. Raise the left heel off the floor but with the toes in contact with the floor. On the second count bring the left foot to a closed position and shift body weight from the right foot (cut). In doing this the left leg is straightened to take the body weight and the right foot raises slightly off the floor with the knee bent and the ankle extended, toes pointing downward. On the third count the left knee is bent in preparation for the hop. As the rising movement begins, the right foreleg starts swinging with the foot moving slightly over the instep of the left foot. On the completion of the hop (left) the right foot has been brought into position with the heel almost against the shinbone of the supporting leg, the ankle extended, and the toes pointing to the floor. In some sections of the United States, in dancing this movement for the Varsouvianna, a small circling action is taken with the ankle and foot as the right foreleg sweeps into position against the left leg.

4. Practice the patterns, verbalizing the actions. Start the gliding step first with the right and then with the left foot. Pay close attention to the closing or cutting step that occurs on the second beat. The body weight must be abruptly displaced to obtain the characteristic action of the Mazurka and Varsouvienne. Practice with music, recognizing the upbeat at the onset of the music but start the pattern on the count of one with the gliding step.

			Hop L			Hop L
Pattern:	Step R	Cut L	Swing R	Step R	Cut L	Swing R
Count:	1	2	3	1	2	3

FOLK DANCES

The following folk dances are organized on a graduated level ranging from simple to complex. They provide an opportunity for performing and practicing the Mazurka and Varsouvienne patterns discussed in this chapter. In describing the dances, credit has been given to the source from which the author first learned the dance.

Varsouvianna (United States)

Formation: This charming dance has almost as many dance positions as it has names. Called La Varsouviana, Put Your Little Foot, and Varsovianna to name but three, it frequently is danced in closed position, semi-open position and Varsouvienne position. In some instances, a double circle of couples is formed. At other times, couples are scattered on the floor moving in a counterclockwise direction. The following dance description is best performed as a couple dance in Varsouvienne position.

Music: Folk Dancer M. H. 3012; Folkraft 1034; Windsor 4615; World of Fun M 107

Meter: 3/4

Source: As taught at a National Health, Physical Education and Recreation Conference in 1956.

Pattern: In 3/4 meter, two basic movement phrases are always present. The long phrase consists of two Varsouvienne patterns followed by three steps and a point. This is repeated at least once and sometimes it is taken three times. The short phrase is so-called in that the action of the third and fourth measures of the long phrase are used. Some versions of the dance have a third phrase of a waltz turn for 8 or 16 measures.

MEASURES

Long Phrase

1—2   Two Varsouvienne patterns moving counterclockwise. Both the man and the woman start with their weight on the right foot. Start the patterns on the upbeat with a lift (raising of the heel) rather than a definite hop on the right foot. Lift right. Swing left (count ah). Step forward left (count 1). Close right to left (count 2).

3—4   Lift right. Swing left (count 3). Girl moves sideward in front of man with 3 steps to his left side. Man takes 3 steps in place (left-right-left). Both point diagonally forward with right foot (counts 1—2—3).

5—8   Repeat action of measure 1—4 in reverse. Start Varsouvienne patterns with lift on left foot and the girl moves sideward right with walking steps.

Short Phrase

9—10   Repeat action of measure 3—4.

11—12   Repeat action of measure 5—8.

13—16   Repeat actions of measure 9—12.

Variation I
Long phrase as described.
Short phrase.

9—10   Right hands dropped. Girl moves forward in a half circle to man's left side facing clockwise with the 3 walking steps and point of measure 3—4. Man takes the patterns in place facing counterclockwise.

11—12   The girl makes a turn under the joined left hands with the 3 walking steps and point to return the man's right side facing counterclockwise. Man takes the pattern in place facing counterclockwise.

13—16   Repeat the action of measure 9—12.

Variation II
Long phrase as described.
Short phrase.

9—14	Repeat the action of measure 9—12 of Variation I.
15—16	Partners drop hands, with 3 walking steps and a forward point of the free foot, the girl moves clockwise and the man moves counterclockwise to progress to a new partner. If the waltz phrase is not included in the music, the girl makes a half turn left with the 3 steps as she progresses to her new partner in order to finish in Varsouvienne position.
	NOTE: A closed dance position is used for the 8 or 16 measures of waltz turns that are made clockwise while progressing in a counterclockwise direction.

Swedish Varsovienne (Sweden)

Formation:	In many respects, this dance is related very closely to the American Varsouvianna. A variety of patterns and dance positions may be used. For the following description, it is recommended that an open dance position be used by couples facing counterclockwise with outside hands on hips, thumb extending backward, fingers extending forward.
Music:	Folk Dancer M. H. 1023
Meter:	3/4
Source:	Originally learned from Swedish folk dance group in New York City.
Pattern:	Walk, mazurka, waltz.
MEASURES	
	Figure I Walking Steps and Heel
1	Starting on outside feet (man's left,

	girl's right) girl crosses in front of partner to his left side with 3 walking steps. Man takes 3 steps almost in place and simultaneously changes arm position so that on the last step, his left arm is around girl's waist and her right hand is on his shoulder, outside hands on hips.
2	Place free foot forward, heel on floor, toe raised slightly (man's right, girl's left).
3—4	Starting with man's right and girl's left repeat action of measure 1—2, returning to original position.
5—8	Repeat action of measure 1—4.

Figure II Mazurka

9—10	Starting on outside feet (man's left, girl's right) take 2 mazurka steps forward moving in a counterclockwise direction. Step forward with slight emphasis (count 1). Close (count 2). Hop, sweeping free foot across shinbone of supporting leg.
11—12	Repeat action of measure 1—2.
13—14	Starting on man's right and girl's left repeat action of measure 9—10.
15—16	Repeat action of measure 3—4.

Figure III Waltz

17—24	In closed dance position, couples take 8 waltz turns, turning clockwise while progressing in a counterclockwise direction.

Black Forest Mazurka (Germany)

Formation:	Couples scattered on floor facing counterclockwise. Inside hands

joined at shoulder height with out-side hands on hips.

Music:	Folk Dancer M. H. 1048
Meter:	3/4
Source:	Originally learned from German folk dance groups in New York City.
Pattern:	Running waltz, mazurka.

MEASURES

Figure I Running Waltz

1—2   Starting on man's left foot and girl's right foot move forward counter-clockwise with 2 running waltz patterns. Joined hands move slightly forward and backward as partners turn slightly away and toward each other.

3   Drop joined hands, complete a full turn away from partner with 1 forward running waltz pattern while continuing to progress in counter-clockwise direction. Man turns left and girl turns right.

4   With 3 short steps continue to move forward counterclockwise and at the same time clap own hands 3 times.

Figure II Mazurka

5—6   In open dance position facing coun-terclockwise take 2 mazurka steps forward starting on outside feet (man's left, girl's right).

7—8   Keeping the open dance position, couple makes one complete circle counterclockwise with 6 running steps. The man, acting as a pivot, takes small steps in a backward direction while the girl circles for-ward with relatively long steps.

Eide Ratas (Estonia)

Formation: Couples in semi-open dance position moving counterclockwise.

Music: Folk Dancer M. H. 1018; Educational Dance Recordings FD-3

Meter: 3/4

Source: Dance arranged from the dance description by Michael Herman. *Folk Dances For All,* New York: Barnes and Noble, Inc., 1947, pp. 86-87.

Pattern: Mazurka, running steps, waltz turns.

MEASURES

Figure I   Mazurka Pattern and Turn

1—2   2 mazurka patterns moving counterclockwise starting on man's left foot and girl's right foot. The first step of each of these mazurka patterns is a forward LEAP (count 1) bending the body forward at the same time. The inside foot is brought sharply forward (count 2) to displace the first step and hop (count 3). On the second and third movements, the body comes to an upright position.

3—4   In place, couple turns clockwise (man forward, girl backward acting as a pivot) with 6 running steps. Complete a full circle.

5—8   Repeat action of measure 1—4.

1—8   Repeat action of measure 1—8.

Figure II   Waltz Turns and Running Steps

9—10   Partners face with own hands on

hips. Man has back to center of room, girl faces toward center of room. Moving AWAY from each other, both beginning on left foot. 1 forward half turn left with waltz pattern. 1 forward half turn right with waltz pattern.

11–12   Repeat action of measure 9–10 continuing to move AWAY from partner. Finish last turn definitely facing partner.

13–14   Partners move forward with 6 running steps toward each other, starting on left foot.

15–16   Hook right elbows and turn once and a half in place with 6 running steps. Finish in opposite positions. Man facing center of room, girl with back to center of the room.

9–16   Repeat action of measure 9–16 but hook left elbows to finish in original positions.

Repeat Figure I and Figure II for measure 17–32.

Kreuz Koenig (Germany)

Formation: Sets of two couples facing. Girl on boy's right side.

Music: Folk Dancer M. H. 1022

Meter: 3/8. The music for Figure III is faster than for any other figure of the dance.

Source: Dance description arranged from description given by Michael Herman. *Folk Dances for All.* New York: Barnes and Noble, Inc., 1947, pp. 90-92.

Pattern: Leap, running steps, step-hop, mazurka.

MEASURES

Figure I   Circling Clockwise

1—2

All hands joined, facing center, starting with left foot. Leap sideward clockwise with left foot (count 1). Cross right in back of left foot (count 2). Step left making a quarter turn to face in a clockwise direction (count 3). 3 forward running steps (right-left-right) (counts 1—2—3).

3—8

Repeat action of measure 1—2 three times.

Figure II   Running Steps in Line of Four

1—8

Men hook left elbows and place right arms around partner's waist. Girls at partners' right side facing in same direction, place left arms across partner's back and join hands (left to left) with opposite man. Girl's right hand placed on top of man's right hand at waist. All starting on the left foot take 24 running steps forward circling counterclockwise.

Figure III   Men Cross Over, Turn and Return

9—12

All hands released, re-form original formation. Starting with left foot, men join left hands and change places with 2 forward step-hop patterns. Step left (count 1—2). Hop left (count 3). Step right (counts 1—2). Hop right (count 3). Men join right hands with opposite girl turning once around her clockwise with 2 forward step-hop patterns. Girls take 4 small step-hop patterns in place.

13—14

Repeat action of measure 9—12.

15

Partners join right hands and girl

with 1 step-hop turns clockwise under uplifted arms while man stands in place.

16   Partners facing. Men bow and girls curtsy.

9—16   Repeat action of measure 9—16.

Figure IV   Circling with Mazurka Pattern

17—20   All join hands, form a circle and face clockwise. 4 mazurka patterns circling clockwise. Start the mazurka pattern with a forward step left (count 1). Close right to left (count 2). Hop left (count 3).

21—22   Partners face and take a two hand hold position. Beginning on left foot, 2 mazurka patterns circling clockwise.

23—24   Continuing to circle clockwise, take 6 running steps (left-right-left-right-left-right) leaning away from partner.

17—24   Re-form circle of four and repeat action of measure 17—24.

Figure V   The King's Cross

Throughout this figure, do not let go of partner's right hand.

25—28   Girls back to back, right to right hands joined with partner, left to left hands joined with opposite man. Men turn slightly clockwise and with 12 forward running steps circle the foursome clockwise. Girls run in place as they pivot in center, kicking feet slightly forward.

29   Men release left hand of opposite girl and with a right to right hand hold with partner swing the girls to outside position as they move to

center and take back to back position. Men rejoin left hands with opposite girl. Take 3 running steps to make this changeover (right-left-right).

30–32

Repeat the action of measure 25–28 with girls circling the foursome clockwise.

25–32

Repeat the action of measure 25–32.

NOTE. At completion of the dance, all hands are dropped and the men turn in place to re-form sets of two couples facing. The man finds his old partner on his left side and the opposite girl on his right side. The dance is repeated with the new partner.

Martinique Mazurka (Island of Martinique, West Indies)

Formation:

Couples in a double circle facing counterclockwise. Inside hands joined. Girl on man's right side. Girl holds skirt in right hand. Man closes left hand and places it backward on hip.

Music:

Folkways FW 6840, Band 2

Meter:

3/4. It is difficult to recognize this music as a Mazurka but when the original Mazurka was imported to the island by French colonists, it became mixed with the music of the Beguine. The 3/4 meter of the Mazurka was superimposed upon the Beguine and results in this dance being performed much more rapidly than most Mazurka dances.

Source:

Lidster, Miriam D., and Tamburini, Dorothy H. *Folk Dance Progressions*. Belmont, California: Wadsworth Publishing Co. Inc., 1965, pp. 252-256.

Pattern: Beguine, mazurka, change step, cross mazurka, mazurka-beguine.

MEASURES

Introduction

1—8   Couples, inside hands joined at shoulder level, sway to music. This, like the entire dance, is performed in a subtle, graceful manner.

Figure I Beguine

1—8   Starting on outside feet (man's left, girl's right) move counterclockwise with 8 beguine steps. Step forward on outside feet (count 1). Cross inside foot in back of outside foot, change weight (count and). Step almost in place on outside foot (count 2). Step on inside foot (count and). Step on outside foot (count 3). On repeating this step, the man would start with his right foot, the girl with her left foot.

Figure II Mazurka and Change

1—7   In open position, outside hands joined, take 7 mazurka steps moving counterclockwise. Begin with outside feet. Step forward on outside foot and incline the body forward (count 1). Rock back onto inside foot straightening the body (count 2). Lift on inside foot (no hop) and brush outside foot slightly across in front of supporting leg (count 3).

8   Beginning on outside feet, 1 change step to face clockwise. Retain open position with outside hands joined. Step back on outside foot (count 1). Step sideward with inside foot (count 2). Step forward with outside foot (between partner's and toward reverse line of direction).

While the change is being made couple shifts direction to face clockwise.

9—16

Starting on man's right foot, girl's left foot, take 7 mazurka steps moving clockwise and 1 change step to finish facing counterclockwise.

Figure III   Repetition

1—8

Repeat action of measure 1—8 of Figure I.

1—16

Repeat action of measure 1—16 of Figure II.

Figure IV   Cross Mazurka

1—2

Partners face, right hands joined and right shoulders adjacent. Take 1 cross mazurka and 1 change step. Man steps sideward left to dance 1 mazurka pattern and 1 change step as described in Figure II. On the change step, left to left hands are joined and left to left shoulders are brought into adjacent positions. The girl crosses right over left and steps forward on right foot (count 1). Steps *back* onto left foot (count 2). Brush right in front of left (count 3). She brings right foot in a circular motion to step *back* on the first step of the change pattern.

3—4

With left hands joined and left to left shoulders adjacent, repeat action of measure 1—2 starting on man's right foot, girl's left foot.

Figure V   Elbows Joined

1—8

With right elbows joined, make 1 complete circle clockwise with 8 beguine steps. Both partners lean in direction of foot used. On the first pattern, man starts with left foot and leans to his left. Girl starts on her right foot and leans to her right.

On the second pattern, starting on opposite feet, man leans right and girl leans left.

9—16   With left elbows joined moving counterclockwise repeat action of measure 1—8 starting with man on right foot, girl on left foot.

Figure VI   Mazurka-Beguine

1—7   Partners face with man's back to center of circle. Starting left, each moves sideward left with 7 mazurka-beguine steps. Step sideward left (count 1). Step onto right in place (count 2). Close left to right (count and). Step right in place (count 3).

8   1 change step starting with left foot.

9—16   Repeat action of measure 1—8 starting with right foot.

Interlude

1   Holding skirt up slightly, girl takes weight on right foot (count 1). Step left back of right (count 2) and inclines body slightly forward to bow to partner. Man, in place, curves right arm in front of body, left arm curved to back, bows to girl.

2—4   Girl repeats bow 3 times stepping left-right-left. Boy repeats bow 3 times in place.

Figure VII   Beguine

1—8   Repeat action of Figure I, measure 1—8.

Figure VIII   Mazurka and Change

1—8   Repeat action of Figure II, measure 1—8.

9—16   Repeat action of Figure II, measure 9—16 to end of music.

CHAPTER 6

THE WALTZ

BACKGROUND

The noted dance authority Curt Sachs maintains that "the roots of all turning dances are lost in the Neolithic vegetation cults." It is possible that this may be the source of the Waltz with its characteristic rotating and revolving movements. Yet, it is not known at what point in history the dance developed or exactly what racial group first performed it. There is no written reference to a dance called Walzer until the 1750's but it is believed that under other names, the pattern was a part or the total movements of other dances.

Many dance historians agree that if there is one major source of the dance, it is most likely to be the German Landler which in turn evolved from the work songs and dances of the people of Bavaria and the Austrian Steiermark. It is known that in these dances wild movements of hopping, stamping, and throwing the female partner into the air were performed. It also has been traced that in the exuberance of participating in such dances, the girl would twist under the raised arms of her partner or both would slip under each other's arms to dance back to back. On turning to face each other, they would closely embrace and joyously whirl and turn. It is this last movement which is credited with producing the dance now called Waltz.

Numerous changes occurred in the Waltz before it became the most popular form of ballroom dancing in the nineteenth century. Separated from the dances in which it was used, it gradually lost many of its coarser features. Moving upward to the polished ballroom floors of Austrian aristocracy, the closed dance position was retained in a more refined form and a set style began to be established for the dance. Frequently, it was performed in combination with the stately and dignified Allemande. Danced in succession, these two dances made a contrasting pair. The graceful Allemande with its 2/4 meter music first would be performed. Moving in a longway set, the dancers would execute a processional series of movements around the ballroom floor. On their completion, the musicians would change to music written in 3/4 meter and the dancers would assume the closed position for the Waltz. Sometimes referred to as the *tripla* (taken from the triple meter of the music) the couples then would whirl rapidly and revolve around the floor at a dizzy pace.

The Waltz apparently led a hidden life for over 150 years. French experts agree that the Waltzer, which they renamed the Valse, came from the Austrian courts and became popular in their country, as in England, during the nineteenth century. They insist, however, that the Volté first performed by their lower class in the sixteenth century contained the same type of turning movements and, therefore, the movements of the Waltz were not new to them. People were either delighted with the fast turning movements or they were shocked and outraged at the indecent positions taken by the dancers. In England particularly there were loud denunciations of the dance and demands were made that it be banned from the ballroom floor. In spite of the protests, the Waltz rapidly assumed the position of being "the queen of ballroom dancing."

When first introduced into this country, the Waltz was received with the same mixed feelings as in England. Some persons enjoyed both watching and performing it. Others feared for the morals and virtues of their own and future generations. It was a number of decades before the Waltz finally acquired the respectable position which it enjoys today. During the first years, it was both bitterly attacked and vigorously defended. Statements frequently appeared in print and, in 1817, one poem best expressed the feelings of both the pro and anti waltz groups.

> . . . They rise, they twirl, they sing, they fly,
> Puffing, blowing, jostling, squeezing
> Very odd, but very pleasing—
> 'Till every Lady plainly shows
> (Whatever else she may disclose)
> Reserve is not among her faults:
> Reader this is (to) the waltz.*

RHYTHMIC COUNT AND STYLE

The basic pattern of the Waltz consists of three movements, step-step-close taken in even rhythm and equally sharing the three beats of a measure of music. For other waltz patterns containing two movements, such as the Step-Arch, Step-Swing, and Step-Draw, the first step most often is given the time value of the accented beat of one, and the action which follows absorbs the second and third beats of the music measure.

---

*Marks, Joseph E., III, *America Learns to Dance*. New York, Exposition Press, 1957, p. 74.

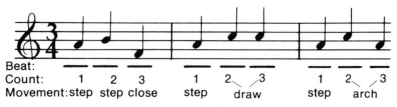

Beat:								
Count:	1	2	3	1	2	3	1	2	3
Movement:	step	step	close	step		draw	step		arch

Over the years, a variety of styles have developed for the Waltz. In some European countries, it is danced on the flat of the foot with a gliding step starting the pattern. In other parts of the world, the body weight is kept on the balls of the feet throughout the pattern with the heels lifted slightly off the floor. In this country, the slower tempo of waltz music has resulted in a style which is uniquely American. In the closed dance position, described and illustrated in Chapter 3, the girl arches her back slightly and leans back lightly against the boy's arm to create graceful line. The curve that she forms resembles a very shallow C. On moving, the action of the steps originates in the hip to give the pattern a smooth and flowing quality. To coincide with the accent occurring on the first beat, the first step is made longer than the two that follow. On the Step-Close taken on the second and third beats of the music measure, a slight up-down action is done by the dancer taking a step (forward, backward or sideward on the count of 2) on the ball of the foot with the heel raised slightly off the floor. On the closing step that follows, body weight first is shifted to the ball of the foot and the heel comes to the floor in preparation for the longer step that will start the next pattern.

SUGGESTED LEARNING PROCEDURES

The rhythm and style of the Waltz can be best understood by first mastering the running waltz pattern. In folk dances, this pattern is taken forward, backward, or circling. Listen to several pieces of waltz music at varying tempos before beginning to practice. Clap and count the three beats of each measure, emphasizing the accented beat of one. Take three steps in place with emphasis on the first step while continuing to clap and count. Once the movements and style of the running waltz pattern are mastered, learn the box pattern taken in place and the turns which are developed from it.

Running waltz pattern

1. Verbalizing the three beats either by counting or by the movements being taken, practice moving forward alone with *Step*-step-close. Be sure that the first step is slightly longer than the two steps that follow and that the movement originates in the hip and not in the knee or foot. As the pattern is repeated several times starting on alternate feet, a smooth, even, continuous action should be felt with a slight up—down feeling on the second and third steps.

Pattern:	*step*	step	close
Style:	long	up	down
Count:	1	2	3

2. Combine forward running with a circling pattern. Take two running waltz patterns to complete a full circle. Then do a forward running pattern starting left and combine it with a circling pattern forward right. Repeat the forward running pattern starting right and complete a full circle to the left.

Pattern:	forward	step	close	circle	step	close	step	step	close
Feet:	left	right	left	right	left	right	left	right	left
Count:	*1*	2	3	*1*	2	3	*1*	2	3

Pattern:	forward	step	close	circle	step	close	step	step	close
Feet:	right	left	right	left	right	left	right	left	right
Count:	*1*	2	3	*1*	2	3	*1*	2	3

3. Practice the forward running waltz and circling right and the circling left with music alone.

4. Take a partner in open position with inside hands joined. Change the combination to two running steps forward and circling away from partner for two measures. (Boy circling forward left, girl circling right.) Start on the outside feet. As the circling patterns begin, joined hands are released and then rejoined as partners face original direction on the last two steps of the next pattern.

In some folk dances, the running waltz pattern is used to progress in one direction by taking one pattern forward and the next pattern backward.

1. Practice this by verbalizing the actions with the music. Step forward left, step forward right, and with weight on the ball of the foot start to pivot right to face the opposite direction. Bring left foot into closed position completing the half turn. To continue moving in the same direction, the next pattern is backward. Step back right, step back left, and with weight on the ball of the foot start to pivot right to face in the original direction. Bring right foot into closed position and complete the half turn. As the half turns are made from a forward and backward pivot action, they are taken in the same direction.

2. Take a Varsouvienne position and partner practice with music. Keep joined hands throughout a series of patterns forward and backward. Start forward left on the same feet. On the completion of the first pattern starting forward, the girl is in a Varsouvienne position at her partner's *left side*. On completing the second pattern starting backward, the girl is back in her original position at her partner's *right side*. This is done as partners pivot and half turn independently with hands held throughout the movements.

Waltz box pattern

The box pattern of the Waltz is done in two patterns consisting of a step, a step sideward, and a closing step. When the first step is taken forward on the first pattern and the first step of the second pattern begins backward (or the opposite way around) the two patterns make a square box.

1. With partners facing but each moving independently, practice the pattern with the boy starting forward on his left foot and the girl stepping backward on her right foot. Verbalize the actions but do not use the words "left" and "right" since the partners are moving on opposite feet.

Pattern:	step	step sideward	close
Count:	1	2	3

An error which frequently occurs when the box pattern first is being learned is the failure to take the body weight on the third or closing step. To correct this mistake, change the verbalization of the movements from Step-step-close to Step-step-*change* making sure that, as the foot comes into the closed position on the third beat, it takes the body weight and becomes the support foot. A second error may occur if the waltz pattern is started in reverse. Step-close-step. This is known as a Two-Step Waltz and can be corrected by taking the first step of each pattern directly forward or backward. As the second step is taken, do not bring it near the supporting leg but instead take it deliberately sideward. Verbalize, emphasizing the closing step which occurs on the third beat. Step-step-*close.*

2. Practice to music with a partner in a closed dance position.

Waltz turns

With the box pattern successfully accomplished, it is easy to learn how to turn to the left and to the right, starting with a forward or backward step, in order to make quarter, alternate, and half turns. Remember in turning that *basically the box pattern is used.*

1. Practicing alone and without music take one box pattern starting forward left. As the left foot comes forward turn the foot outward (toe out) and twist your upper body in the direction your foot is pointing, to turn to the left. (The step sideward and the closing step on the counts of two and three do not assist in making the turn. They *complete it by reducing the distance which the dancer wishes to turn.*) For example, in a quarter turn the step sideward and the closing step would cut out one-fourth of a full circle. If the dancer wishes to turn further, he would do so by taking a slightly longer step forward on the first beat of music, twisting the upper body more and, with the step sideward and the closing step, completing a 120 degree turn (a third of the circle) or a 180 degree turn (a half of the circle). Practice

making different degrees of turns to the left by taking the left foot forward and toeing out with a slightly longer or shorter step and with a twisting action in the body.

2. Using the backward portion of the box pattern, step backward on the right foot, turn it in so that it is pointing to the left, twist the shoulders and upper body in the direction that the foot is pointing (left), and practice various degrees of turns which can be made to the left starting backward off the right foot.

3. Reverse the position of the feet in the box pattern, start with the right foot forward and the toe out. Twist the upper body in the direction that the foot is pointing, and practice various degrees of turns which can be made to the right, starting forward with the right foot.

4. Take the left foot backward and toe it in so that it is pointing to the right, twist the upper body in the direction that the foot is pointing, and practice various degrees of turns which can be made to the right starting backward off the left foot.

In practicing turns that start either with a forward step or with a backward step, several points quickly become apparent. To turn to the left, the left foot must step forward and toe out on the first step of the waltz pattern or the right foot must step backward on the first step and toe in. To turn to the right, the opposite direction of the feet is needed. The right foot must take the forward step and toe out and the left foot must take the first step in a backward direction and toe in. A second point which also becomes obvious is that the degree of the turn which the dancer wishes to make depends on the length of the first step forward or backward and the amount of twisting action occurring in the shoulders and upper body. The sideward step and the closing step taken on the second and third beats complete but do not assist in making the turn. An error which frequently occurs in learning to turn is the failure of the dancer to take a direct forward or backward step before turning the foot outward or pointing it in. If the foot is taken sideward or on a forward or backward diagonal, it is extremely difficult and sometimes impossible to turn.

5. Practice making several turns to the left. On the first pattern bring the left foot forward and toe out and on the second pattern continue to turn left by bringing the right foot backward and toeing it in. *The box step is being used* with the addition of the toeing out and toeing in on the first step of each pattern. Practice making a series of left turns in quarters, and in thirds (completing a full circle with three turns) and in halves.

6. Repeat the practice making the turns to the right.

7. Practice a series of turns to the left and then to the right starting with a backward step.

8. With a partner in closed dance position as explained in Chapter 3, practice several quarter turns, one-third turns and half turns to the left. Repeat the same practice making several successive turns of varying degrees to the right. Apply and practice the principles of leading and following as explained in Chapter 3.

Alternate turns

In many folk dances using the Waltz pattern, couples progress in some one direction using waltz turns. In some instances, half turns must be used since a certain direction for turning is stipulated. For example, "using waltz turns, couples turn clockwise as the large circle revolves counterclockwise." In other dances, the instructions for turning and progressing are not as specific. They may only indicate that couples are to move with waltz turns in a counterclockwise direction around the room. When dancers participate in this type of free ballroom dancing, progressive turns can be more successfully accomplished by alternating the direction of the turns and a relatively straight line progression can be accomplished by alternating the way of turning from left to right and from right to left.

To do this, three turns are made to the left (or right) to complete a full circle. Each turn is 120 degrees or a one-third turn. On completing the third turn, the couple is facing in the original direction with the opposite foot free. A second series of three turns to complete a full circle is then taken to the right (or left) in *exactly the same way.* Thus, if the first series of turns starts with a *forward* left turn, the second series also starts with a *forward* turn.

First series — three turns to the left:

	turn			turn			turn	
Pattern: forward	step-close	backward	step-close	forward	step-close
Feet:	L	R	L	R	L	R	L	R	L
Count:	1	2	3	1	2	3	1	2	3

Second series — three turns to the right:

	turn			turn			turn	
Pattern: forward	step-close	backward	step-close	forward	step-close
Feet:	R	L	R	L	R	L	R	L	R
Count:	1	2	3	1	2	3	1	2	3

1. With music, practice alternate turns alone, starting with a series that begins with a forward left turn, and add to this a second series of turns (3 turns) that start with a forward right turn. Reverse the sequence and start with a series of turns to the right and add a series of turns to the left. Remember that each turn must cut out approximately one third of a circle and on completing the third turn, your are facing in your original direction.

2. Continue to practice alone making several series of turns that

start with backward turns starting with the right and then with the left foot.

3. Take a partner in a closed dance position and applying the principles of leading and following take alternate turns that start forward left for the boy (as well as starting backward off his right foot). Reverse the directions in which the series of turns start to the right. Practice first with music at a relatively slow speed. As the skill of alternate turning is acquired, gradually increase the speed of the music.

One of the most common errors in learning alternate turns is the failure of the boy to make turns which equally divide a circle into three parts. Frequently, he will substitute quarter turns and fail to complete a full circle in three turns, or he will correctly turn forward but fail to take any turn on a backward pattern. To correct this fault, he should select three objects in the room which are approximately 120 degrees apart. On completing each turn in a series left or right, he should check and see if he is in line with the first, the second, and the third object.

FOLK DANCES

The following folk dances are organized on a graduated level ranging from simple to complex. They provide an opportunity for performing and practicing the Waltz patterns discussed in this chapter. In describing the dances, credit has been given to the source from which the author first learned the dance.

Tu Ting (Denmark)

Formation:	Couples scattered on floor moving counterclockwise. Open dance position with inside hands joined, outside hands on hips.
Music:	Folk Dancer M. H. 1018; Educational Dance Recordings FD-2; RCA FAS 664
Meter:	3/4, 2/4
Source:	Learned by author in New York City, 1946.
Pattern:	Waltz, walking step.

MEASURES

3/4 meter	**Figure I Waltz Step Forward and Turning**
1−4	Starting on outside feet (man's left, girl's right) move counterclockwise with 4 forward waltz steps, turning slightly away from each other on the first and third patterns with joined hands swinging forward and on the second and fourth patterns turning toward each other with joined hands swinging backward.
5−8	In closed dance position, 4 waltz turns clockwise while progressing in a counterclockwise direction. Boy starts with a backward turn to the right.
1−8	Repeat action of measure 1−8.
2/4 meter	**Figure II Walking Steps and Pivot**
9−12	Open dance position with outside hands on hips. Starting on outside feet (man's left, girl's right) take 4 forward walking steps counterclockwise.
13−16	Shoulder-waist position. Take a pivot, turn in place with 4 walking steps.
9−16	Repeat action of measure 9−16.

Kehruu Valssi or Spinning Waltz (Finland)

Formation:	Couples in double circle facing with both hands joined. Boys have their backs to the center of the circle.
Music:	Imperial 1036; World of Fun M 110; MacGregor 607
Meter:	3/4

Source: Learned at National Health, Phys-
                                     ical Education and Recreation Con-
                                     ference, 1956.

Pattern: Waltz, balance, walking step.

MEASURES

                                     **Figure I   Step-Swing, Walking
                                     Steps, and Turn**

1 – 2   Moving sideward (boy's left, girl's
                                     right). Step (count 1). Swing free
                                     foot across supporting leg (counts
                                     2 – 3). Repeat to opposite side.

3 – 4   Moving sideward left, boy takes 3
                                     steps and swings. Step left (counts
                                     1 – 2). Step right (count 3). Step left
                                     (count 1). Swing right (counts 2 – 3).

                                     Girl turning clockwise and progress-
                                     ing with partner takes 3 steps. Step
                                     right (counts 1 – 2). Step left (count
                                     3). Step right (count 1) and finishes
                                     facing partner with left foot swing-
                                     ing across supporting leg (counts
                                     2 – 3).

5 – 6   Repeat action of measure 1 – 2 with
                                     boy starting on right foot, girl on left
                                     foot.

7 – 8   Repeat action of measure 3 – 4 with
                                     patterns reversed. Girl steps side-
                                     ward with 3 steps and swings, boy
                                     takes clockwise turn.

                                     Figure II   Balance and Turn

9 – 10   Partners facing with two hands
                                     joined. 1 balance step forward (boy
                                     starting left, girl right). Arms swing
                                     outward. 1 balance step backward.
                                     Arms return to position.

11 – 12   Moving forward so that right shoul-
                                     ders are adjacent and joined hands
                                     are extended sideward shoulder

	height, turn clockwise with 6 forward walking steps. Finish in original position.
13 – 14	Repeat action of measure 9 – 10.
15 – 16	Facing counterclockwise with outside hands joined. Man progresses forward with 2 running waltz steps while girl takes 2 waltz turns clockwise while progressing with partner in counterclockwise direction.
	NOTE: On measure 15 – 16, the man could take 6 steps in place while girl progresses forward with turns to new partner.

Black Hawk Waltz (United States)

Formation:	Couples in closed dance position moving counterclockwise.
Music:	Folk Dancer M. H. 3002; Folkraft 1046
Meter:	3/4
Source:	Learned in Los Angeles in 1961.
Pattern:	Waltz, balance, cross waltz.
MEASURES	
	Figure I Balance and Quarter Turns
1 – 2	In place, boy takes 1 balance step forward left (girl, backward right) and 1 balance step backward right (girl, forward left).
3 – 4	Repeat actions of measure 1 – 2.
5 – 8	Boy starting forward left takes 4 quarter turns to left with waltz pattern. Finish facing in line of direction. Girl takes counterpart.

9−16	Repeat action of measure 1−8.

Figure II   Cross Waltz and Point

17−18	Facing partner in two hand hold position or closed position. Boy crosses left over right (counts 1−2−3). Crosses right over left (counts 1−2−3). Girl does counterpart.
19−20	Moving in reverse line of direction, boy crosses left over right (counts 1−2−3). Steps sideward right with right foot (count 1). Crosses left in back of right (count 2). Points right foot sideward right (count 3). Girl does counterpart.
21−24	Repeat action of measure 17−20 with boy starting on right foot, girl on left foot.
25−32	Repeat action of measure 17−24.

Oslo Waltz (Scotland-England)

Formation:	Single circle with partners facing center. All hands joined. Girl on right side of man.
Music:	Folk Dancer M. H. 3016
Meter:	3/4
Source:	Krause, Richard, *Folk Dancing.* New York, The Macmillan Co., 1962, p. 146.
Pattern:	Balance, running waltz, step-draw, waltz turns, step-swing.

MEASURES

Figure I   Balance and Running Waltz

1−2	All do a waltz balance forward (man starts on left foot, girl on right) and a waltz balance backward.

3—4

Man releases partner's hand but continues to hold right hand of girl on his left side. With 2 running waltz steps, she crosses over in front of him stepping backward on the last step to face center on right side of man.

5—8

Repeat action of measure 1—4.

9—16

Repeat action of measure 1—8. On completion of last running steps, girl has passed to the right four times.

Figure II   Step-Swing and Turn

1—2

Man faces new partner and joins both hands. 1 step-swing pattern toward center of circle, 1 step-swing pattern away from center. Step sideward (count 1). Swing free foot across supporting foot (counts 2—3). Man starts sideward left, girl starts sideward right.

3—4

Drop hands and partners make a complete circle away from each other with 1 waltz turn and 2 steps. Hold the last count of measure 4. Man turns counterclockwise starting with left foot. Girl turns clockwise starting with right foot. On turn, progression is made toward center of circle.

5—8

Partners facing and both hands joined, repeat action of measure 1—4, Figure II, in reverse direction. Man starts on right foot. Girl starts on left foot.

Figure III   Step-Draw and Step-Arch, Waltz Turns

9—10

Facing partner, join both hands. 1 step-draw and 1 step-arch toward center (see Glossary). Man starts sideward left, girl starts sideward right.

11–12	Repeat action of measure 1–2, Figure III, in reverse. Man starts sideward right, girl starts sideward left. On last step-arch, partners turn slightly so that man finishes with his back to the center of the circle.
13–14	In closed dance position, take 2 waltz turns clockwise while progressing in counterclockwise direction. Man starts with a backward turn to the right.
15–16	As man faces center and steps in place, girl turns with 6 steps under joined hands (man's left, girl's right).

Sudmalinas (Latvia)

Formation:	Sets of two couples facing. Girl on right side of man.
Music:	RCA Victor LPM 1621
Meter:	2/4, 3/4
Source:	Dance arranged from dance description by Michael Herman Folk Dance House, New York, N. Y.
Pattern:	Polka, Waltz.

MEASURES

2/4 meter	**Figure I Circle and Clap**
1–6	All join hands and move counterclockwise with 6 polka steps. Start with hop on left foot.
7–8	Drop joined hands and clap own hands 3 times. Clap (count 1). Clap (count 2). Clap (count 1). Hold (count 2).
1–8	Repeat action of measure 1–8 circling clockwise. Start with hop on right foot.

Figure II   Polka Turns

9—16

Shoulder-waist position. Each couple moves around the other couple in the set with 8 polka steps turning clockwise but progressing counterclockwise.

9—16

Continue actions of measure 9—16 and finish in original positions.

Figure III   Right and Left Hand Mill

17—22

All extend right arms, facing clockwise and join right hands holding them high. Take 6 forward polka steps circling clockwise, starting with hop on left foot.

23—24

Drop mill position and clap own hands 3 times.

17—24

Repeat action of measure 17—24 in reverse forming a left hand mill and moving counterclockwise. Start with hop on left foot.

3/4 meter

25—32 repeated

Figure IV   Waltz

Each man takes the girl opposite him as his new partner and, in closed dance position, they waltz in any direction for 16 waltz steps. When waltz figure ends, each couple should be near another couple so as to exchange partners for repeat of dance.

CHAPTER 7

THE POLKA

BACKGROUND

Many stories have been told of the beginnings of this gay and rollicking Czechoslovakian dance which acquired widespread popularity in Europe and America during the 1840's. One tells of a young peasant girl who, singing her own accompaniment, spontaneously started dancing the Polka one day in the streets of a small town located near the Elbe River. Some truth may exist in this legend but it is doubtful that Anna Chadimova (Slezak) can be credited with originating either the music or the dance. Many historians believe that, as a servant girl moving from place to place, Anna most likely heard the music or saw the dancing in the eastern part of the country. This belief is strengthened by an essay written in 1835 by Jaroslav Langer. Writing on this rural area for a Prague periodical, he mentions the 2/4 meter music that was being played at social gatherings and the variety of steps which people were dancing to it.

The type of music associated with the Polka has changed very little in form since the early years of the 1800's. The dance, however, has changed many times. The alterations made in the step pattern has resulted, as Curt Sachs states, "in only a poor remnant of the dance currently existing." In its first years, the Polka had ten figures which were performed as a song-dance. The songs were translations of the Polish "Cracoviacs," a form of poetry. The meter of the verses exactly fit the beat of polka music. Standing in front of the musicians, one dancer would sing the first half of a stanza which would be repeated by the other dancers. The last half of the stanza would then be sung in the same manner. Dancing would follow and on completion of a figure, the entire action would be repeated with another verse and quite often with another singer. The many steps and patterns used to perform the variety of figures were not new. They were combinations of the *fleuret*, the *pas de bourrée*, and the *schottische* with which the people were well acquainted.

The name Polka cannot be accurately traced to one source. Some dance authorities believe that the word is a corruption of the Czech word *pulka* meaning "half," which is indicative of the short, quick steps that characterize the dance pattern. Other historians reject this source. They recognize the Czech word *polka* meaning "Polish girl" as being the true name and base their beliefs on two facts. First, the Polish verses which were an integral part of the dance. Second, the tremendous sympathy and loyalty which the Czech people were known to have had for the Poles during their revolution of 1831.

During the last years of the 1830's, Henri Cellarius introduced the Polka to Parisian society. It quickly caught the fancy of the peasant as well as the aristocracy and within a short time a "polka-mania" developed. On village greens and in stately ballrooms, the music and dance dominated the social scene. The polka mania steadily grew and during the 1840's spread like an epidemic to other European countries and to America. It was not the Czechoslovakian dance that such popular stage stars as Fanny Elssler and fiery Marie Guy Stephens were demonstrating and that people were dancing. It was a mixture of steps and patterns mainly designed by dancing masters in Prague as well as in Paris.

The giddy, whirling Polka was first seen in America on the stage of the National Theatre in New York City. Dancing master L. de-Garmo Brockes and his 15-year-old partner, Mary Ann Gannon, introduced the dance on May 10, 1844, and the "polka craze" was started. It upset the relatively staid forms of ballroom dancing being performed and people flocked to dancing schools to learn the latest steps of the dance. Although the majority of people thoroughly enjoyed both the music and the dance, there were some who were shocked by the rowdy actions of the dancers and tried to have the dance banned in public places. The immense popularity of the Polka overrode their objections and at social gatherings, it was the "darling of the ballroom floor."

The enthusiastic reception which first greeted the Polka did not last for too long a time. It was an exhausting dance due to the speed of the accompanying music and gradually it began to disappear. It did not, however, completely fade from the social scene. It took its place in American folk dancing and in the 1940's briefly reappeared as a ballroom dance. American "G.I.'s" returning from duty in the European Theatre of World War II "discovered" it in small villages and towns and brought it home with them. Momentarily it regained its popularity with such music as the "Beer Barrel Polka."

RHYTHMIC COUNT AND STYLE

Polka music is written in 2/4 meter with an upbeat at the beginning of the music which gives impetus to the hop that usually starts the dance pattern. As the music progresses from one measure to the next, the last count of each measure (and) takes the place of the upbeat (ah).

Beat:	—	—	—	—	—
Count:	ah	1 and	2 and	1 and	2 and
Movement:	hop	step close	step hop	step close	step hop

A half century ago, the music accompanying the polka was played at a relatively slow speed and this still is true in a few European countries. In most sections of Europe and in America, however, the pattern is associated with music played at a fast speed which requires the dancers to move with short, quick steps.

There are many different types of polka steps and the style in which these patterns are performed varies extensively from country to country and even from one section of a country to another. In Lithuania and the Scandinavian countries, for example, there is no hop used in the pattern. Three small running steps are taken with a hold or pause replacing the hopping action. In some parts of Switzerland, Germany, and Czechoslovakia, the polka is danced as a two step. The Polish people, noted for their very distinctive form, dance the polka with an accentuated hop which sometimes takes the form of a jump. In this country, the polka also assumes a variety of styles depending upon the heritage of the group which is dancing and the region of the country in which they live. In some sections, it is performed in a relatively quiet manner with an easy lift on the upbeat taking the place of a decided hop. In other areas, the polka pattern assumes a boisterous, bouncy quality which the dancers create with a definite hop followed by three short steps taken on the balls of the feet.

SUGGESTED LEARNING PROCEDURES

The rhythmic coordination necessary to perform the polka successfully can be acquired in several different ways. Actually, there is no one method that is completely successful and it is very possible that it will be necessary to try two or more methods before the polka can be correctly danced to the fast speed of the music. The sequence of movements which form the polka pattern may be developed through the slide, the gallop, or by recognizing the movement relationship between the polka and the schottische. Regardless of the method which is selected, it is strongly recommended that, when first learning the pattern, practice be without musical accompaniment until such time as the mechanics of the movement are well learned. It is essential to hear the music and recognize the speed at which the pattern must be executed. The speed, however, can and often does cause confusion. It is not a sound procedure to slow down polka music for learning purposes. By doing so, the music loses its lilting, rollicking quality but more important, a slow tempo does not permit the dancer to acquire a true kinesthetic feeling of the rhythmic relationship which exists between the music when properly played and the movements of the pattern.

When the polka pattern is first being practiced, verbalization of the actions being taken or of the measure count should accompany the dancer in place of music. Beginning with rhythmic counting or action verbalization at a speed which permits the correct execution of the movements, the vocal speed should gradually be increased as the learner gains confidence in what he is doing. When the polka pattern emerges as the final product of the approach through the slide, gallop, two step, or schottische, the verbal accompaniment *should be equal in speed to the piece of music that then will be used for practice.*

Approach from a slide

1. Dancing alone, start with the right foot and move sideward with four sliding steps.

Verbalize:	step	CLOSE	step	CLOSE	step	CLOSE	step	CLOSE
Foot:	right	left	right	left	right	left	right	left

2. Repeat the four sliding steps starting with the left foot and continue to verbalize emphasizing the *close* action.

3. Repeat the actions of 1 and 2 using two sliding steps starting right and two sliding steps starting left.

4. Combine the two sliding steps starting right with the two slides starting left continuing to move in the same direction. To do this a changeover step is needed on the second sliding step of each sequence. On the second slide, take the sideward step but replace the closing step by swinging the free foot forward and turning the body half-way around. The foot that stepped sideward and is supporting the body weight takes a slight hop to assist in making the half turn.

Verbalize:	Right	close	step	CHANGE	Left	close	step	CHANGE
Count:	1	and	2	and	1	and	2	and

5. Continue practicing these movements until the changeover from sliding right to sliding left can be performed without difficulty.

6. Take a partner (girl on boy's right) and in a face-to-face position with arms outstretched and the palms of the hands touching, move in a counterclockwise direction. Repeat the actions of 4. Start with the boy's left foot and the girl's right foot. On the first changeover, the boy's left hand and the girl's right hand are dropped, and the opposite hands swing forward to assist in taking the partially back-to-back position in which the next sequence of sliding steps is taken, starting with the boy's right foot and the girl's left foot. In changing

from a back-to-back position to resume the facing position, the joined hands (boy's right, girl's left) swing backward as the free foot swings and the hop is taken to turn the body. The free hands once again make contact as the sliding steps are taken in a face-to-face position. Verbalize the movements rhythmically but change the emphasis from:

step-close; step CHANGE

Verbalize:	step-close		step-HOP		step-close		step-HOP	
Count:	1	and	2	*and*	1	and	2	*and*

7. Start the pattern with the HOP on the boy's right foot and the girl's left foot and repeat 6. This is the polka step and first by verbalizing and then with music, practice moving around a large circle counterclockwise.

Verbalize:	HOP	step-close		step-HOP		step-close		step-HOP	
Count:	*and*	1	and	2	*and*	1	and	2	*and*

Approach from a gallop

1. Moving alone and starting with the right foot take four gallop steps forward. Stop, change feet and take four gallop steps starting with the left foot. The gallop step (an old dance step called the "galopade") consists of a forward-closing action with the same foot continuously remaining in the forward position.

2. Combine the four forward gallop steps right with the four forward gallop steps left. On the fourth pattern (right or left) change-over by substituting a forward swing of the free foot for the closing step and a slight hop on the supporting foot.

Verbalize:	Right	close	step	close	step	close	step	CHANGE
	Left	close	step	close	step	close	step	CHANGE

3. Combine two gallop steps with the right foot forward with two gallop steps having the left foot forward.

Verbalize:	Right	close	step	CHANGE
	Left	close	step	CHANGE

4. Repeat 3 with a short forward step and with greater emphasis on the hop that occurs on the changeover.

Verbalize:	step-close		step-HOP		step-close		step-HOP	
Count:	1	and	2	*and*	1	and	2	*and*

5. Start the movements with the HOP on the left foot and with music practice the polka pattern moving forward in a direct line.

Actions:	HOP	step-close		step-HOP		step-close		step-HOP	
Count:	*and*	1	and	2	*and*	1	and	2	*and*

6. Practice with a partner in open position, inside hands joined. Partners start on outside feet.

Approach from a schottische

In many respects, the polka and the schottische patterns are alike. They both use three steps and a hop. The major difference mechanically exists in the manner in which they are related to the music. The schottische pattern taken to four beats of a measure of music has the three steps and the hop each taken on a beat of music. The polka, starting on the upbeat with the hop, must share four movements with the two beats of a measure of music.

1. With a partner in open position, inside hands joined, take a series of schottische steps forward starting on the outside foot. Shorten the length of the forward steps and use the traditional style on the hopping portion of the pattern.

2. Increase the speed of the movements and verbally emphasize the HOP.

Pattern:	step	step	step	HOP		step	step	step	HOP
Count:	1	2	3	4		1	2	3	4

3. Start counting from the HOP. Change the verbalization of the count to the 2/4 meter of polka music.

Pattern:	HOP	step	step	step	HOP	step	step	step	HOP
Count:	*and*	1	and	2	*and*	1	and	2	*and*

Polka turns

Although some folk dances require the use of the polka pattern moving forward in some type of side-by-side position, it is most frequently used with couples in a shoulder-waist position (polka position) or in a closed dance position with progression on the floor being made by turning. To turn and progress successfully, it is essential that the principles of leading and following and the fundamentals of turning be understood and applied. If the waltz turns already have been learned, the knowledge and skill acquired in that area easily can be transferred to learning how to turn with the polka pattern.

1. Practicing alone, use a two step pattern (step-close-step). Step forward on the left foot and point it or toe it outward. Twist the shoulders and the upper part of the body as the step is taken. Close with the right foot and step forward again with the left foot toeing out. Continue to turn to the left on the next pattern by bringing the right foot back and pointing it or toeing it inward. Close with the left foot and step backward again with the right foot *toeing in*.

Turning forward left

Pattern: Step forward left, toe out
Close right foot to left
Step forward left, toe out

Turning backward to the left

Pattern: Step backward right, toe in
      Close left foot to right
      Step backward right, toe in

2. Add the hop at the beginning of each two step pattern to form the polka step. But remember that the turning movement is created not *with the hop* but by toeing the foot outward or inward on the *single steps of the pattern* and by twisting the shoulders and upper body in the direction of the turn.

3. Once the principles of turning have been mastered, practice a series of turns in that direction. Practice first rhythmically, verbalizing the action and then use music. Stop for a moment after making four turns in succession (forward, backward, forward, backward) since it is possible to get dizzy.

4. Repeat 1 and practice turning to the right.

Turning forward right

Pattern: Step forward right, toe out
      Close left foot to right
      Step forward right, toe out

Turning backward to the right

Pattern: Step backward left and toe in
      Close right to left
      Step backward left and toe in

5. Repeat 2 and 3 making the turns to the right.

6. To start turning from a backward step, the instructions in 1 and 4 are still pertinent. Remember that in turning backward, the right foot going back on the single steps toes in and, since it is pointing left, creates a left turn. The left foot going back on the single steps and toes in, points to the right and therefore results in a right turn. Practice a series of turns that start with a hop on the left foot and a backward step on the right foot (left turn). The same turns are being made as for a forward turn except that the patterns are reversed.

Turning backward to the left

Pattern: Hop left
          Step backward right and toe in
          Close left to right
          Step backward right and toe in

Turning forward left

Pattern: Hop right
            Step forward left and toe out
            Close right to left
            Step forward left and toe out.

7. Practice a series of turns starting with a backward turn to the right. The hop is taken on the right foot and left foot is then taken back and toed in.

When the neuro-muscular coordination is acquired for turning starting with a forward as well as a backward turn, take a shoulder-waist position with a partner and practice first with rhythmic verbalization of the count or actions (do not use the words left or right). Then practice with verbalization and music and finally with the music alone. In using the shoulder-waist position, the boy stands tall with his arms extended but not stiff and with his hands placed firmly on the two sides of his partner's waist. The girl places her extended arms on the boy's shoulders and with continued light pressure pushing against her partner's shoulders, creates a slight curve in her back from the waist to the shoulders. In this position, as in the closed dance position which follows, it is essential that the principles of leading and following be applied and practiced.

1. With partner, moving in a large counterclockwise circle, take three turns to the left starting with a forward turn for the boy and complete a full circle. Stop and then repeat the turns to the right, again starting with a forward turn for the boy. Be sure that a complete circle is made on the completion of the third turn and that partners are facing in their original direction.

2. Combine the three turns to the left with the three turns to the right. The boy will start each series of turns with a forward turn and the girl doing the counterpart will start each series with a backward turn. Notice that the first and third patterns of *each series* (left and right) *are turns in the same direction.* To progress, it is essential that a full circle be completed with each series of three turns to the left and to the right.

3. Moving in a large counterclockwise circle, practice progressing with the turns left and right, with the boy starting from a backward turn and the girl from a forward turn.

Many folk dances require the polka turns to start from a double circle position with partners facing. Establish this formation with several other couples. To revolve counterclockwise in the large circle with couples turning clockwise, the boys who are standing with their backs to the center of the circle move on the first hop on right foot almost into a single circle facing clockwise. On the step that follows (left foot) they start making a backward half-turn completing it on the last step of the pattern. To continue turning clockwise while the large circle rotates counterclockwise, the half-turns are continued to the right.

To perform polka turns successfully requires a great deal of practice. One of the most common errors which occurs in learning the pattern happens when the dancers in the excitement of moving rapidly forget that on the hop, *the body weight must return to the same foot.* To correct this mistake, it is necessary to return to the verbalization of the movements at a speed slower than the music and once again rebuild the proper muscular coordination.

FOLK DANCES

The following folk dances are organized on a graduated level ranging from simple to complex and provide an opportunity for practicing the Polka patterns discussed in this chapter. In describing the dances, credit has been given to the source from which the author first learned the dance.

Cotton Eyed Joe (United States)

Formation:	Couples scattered on floor, moving in a counterclockwise direction in closed dance position.
Music:	Imperial 1045, Educational Dance Recordings FD-3
Meter:	2/4
Source:	Traditional.
Pattern:	Heel-toe, push step, polka. This dance frequently is performed with a two step rather than with the polka pattern.

MEASURES

Figure I Heel-Toe and Polka

1—2   Touch heel sideward (count 1). Touch toe to heel of supporting foot (count 2). 1 polka step sideward. Man uses left foot for heel and toe and takes polka step sideward left. Girl does counterpart.

3—4

Repeat action of measure 1—2 in reverse line of direction starting right foot for man, left foot for girl.

5—8

Partners drop hands and with 4 polka steps make a complete individual circle. Man circles left, girl circles right.

Figure II Push Step Counterclockwise and Clockwise

9—12

Partners facing. No hands joined. Take 4 push steps (see Glossary) moving counterclockwise. Quickly reverse direction and take 4 push steps clockwise.

13—16

Shoulder-waist position take 4 polka steps turning clockwise while progressing in a counterclockwise direction. Man starts with hop on right foot and makes a backward turn to the right.

Kalvelis (Lithuania)

Formation:

Single circle of couples, facing center, all hands joined. Girl on right side of man.

Music:

Folk Dancer M. H. 1016, Educational Dance Recordings FD-3

Meter:

2/4

Source:

Learned at Lithuanian Dance Festival, New York City.

Pattern:

Polka.

MEASURES

Figure I Circling Counterclockwise and Clockwise

1—7

Starting with hop on left foot, turn body slightly in counterclockwise

	direction and take 7 forward polka steps.
8	Stamp 3 times (right-left-right). Stamp (count 1). Stamp (count and). Stamp (count 2). Hold (count and). While stamping turn body slightly to face clockwise.
1−8	Repeat action of measure 1−8 circling clockwise.

Chorus

9−10	Facing partner, each person claps his own left hand in his right (count 1). Claps his own right in his left (count 2). Repeat left-right.
11−12	Hook right elbows with partner and change places with 2 polka steps.
13−16	Repeat action of measure 9−12. Hook left elbows for polka steps and return to original position.
9−16	Repeat action of measure 9−16.

Figure II Girls to Center, Boys the Same

1−3	Single circle all facing center. Girls move forward with 3 polka steps toward center of the circle. Start with a hop on right. Boys stand in place.
4	Girls with 3 stamping steps face outward.
5−8	Girls move back to place with 3 polka steps and 3 stamps.
1−8	Repeat action of measure 1−3, Figure III, with men moving to center of circle and out while girls stand in place.
9−16 repeated	Repeat action of Chorus.

Figure III   Grand Right and Left

1—8 repeated

Partners face and join right hands. With 16 polka steps do a Grand Right and Left around circle. Men moving counterclockwise. Girls moving clockwise.

NOTE: If music is not completed when partners get back to original places, partners should hook right elbows and take a polka turn clockwise in place. If the circle is large, partners should meet on the opposite side of the circle.

9—16 repeated

Repeat action of Chorus.

Figure IV   Polka

1—8 repeated

In closed dance position, polka counterclockwise around the room.

9—16 repeated

Partners may continue to polka or they may repeat the action of the Chorus.

Doudlebska Polka (Czechoslovakia)

Formation:

Couples scattered on floor moving counterclockwise in closed dance position.

Music:

Educational Dance Recordings FD-2; Folk Dancer M. H. 3016

Meter:

2/4

Source:

Dance description arranged from Folk Dance House outline.

Pattern:

Polka, walking steps.

MEASURES

Figure I   Polka

1—8

Couples take 8 polka steps turning clockwise while progressing counterclockwise.

| 9 – 16 | Continue the action of measure 1 – 8 moving closer together so that on last polka step a double circle facing counterclockwise can be formed. |

Figure II   Circle and Walk

| 17 – 32 | In open position facing counterclockwise. Man extends left arm forward and places left hand on left shoulder of man in front of him. Take 32 walking steps circling counterclockwise and everyone sings. Tra-la-la, la la la la la, etc. |

Figure III   Ladies Circle Clockwise, Men Clap

| 33 – 48 | Men face to center of circle and clap hands. Clap own hands 2 times (count 1 and). Clap hands of men on both sides (count 2 and). This is repeated throughout the figure. Girls turn and face clockwise and take 16 polka steps circling in a clockwise direction. On the last pattern, girls step behind a man, man turns around, and dance begins again. |

NOTE: During Figure III, extra men or women can join the dance.

Raski-Jaak (Estonia)

Formation:	Line of three facing counterclockwise. Boy between two girls with inside hands joined. Girls outside hands at sides.
Music:	Folk Dancer M. H. 3007
Meter:	2/4
Source:	Dance description arranged from description given by Folk Dance House.
Pattern:	Balance, polka.

MEASURES	
	Chorus
1—4	All balance sideward left starting with left foot. All balance sideward right starting with right foot. Repeat left-right.
5—8	Starting on left foot, 3 walking steps forward kicking right foot forward on last step. Repeat action moving backward starting on right foot.
	Figure I Arches, Over and Under
9—12	With 4 polka steps (short and bouncy) girl on left side goes under the arch formed by right-hand girl and man as the same time girl on the right crosses to opposite side. Continuing to move forward in back of man, girl on the right goes under the arch formed by left-hand girl and man while left-hand girl goes to the outside. Finish in original positions. Man faces counterclockwise and takes the 4 polka steps in place, raising joined hands high over his head.
13—16	Repeat action of measure 9—12.
	Chorus
1—8	Repeat action of measure 1—8.
	Figure II Forward and Backward, Clumping
9—12	With 1 polka step, man swings both girls in front of him so that they face toward him. The girls place their free hand on top of the hand joined with man's to "clump." 3 polka steps forward for the man, backward for the girls.

13 – 16	Reversing the action of measure 9 – 12, man moves backward with 3 polka steps as girls move forward. On the fourth pattern, girls with 1 polka step are swung back into line of 3.
	Chorus
1 – 8	Repeat action of measure 1 – 8.
	Figure III Forward and Backward, Cuddling
9 – 12	With 1 polka step, the man pulls both arms downward and back to turn girls into the curves of his arms facing with him. The joined hands are retained. While doing this, the girls raise their outside arms high. 3 polka steps forward.
13 – 16	Reversing the action of measure 9 – 12, 3 polka steps are taken backward and the girls with 1 polka step are swung back into the line of 3 to start dance again with Chorus.

Kohanochka (Russia)

Formation:	Couples in open position, inside hands joined, moving counterclockwise. Outside arms swing freely with body movements.
Music:	Educational Dance Recordings FD-4; Folk Dancer M. H. 1058; Imperial 1021
Meter:	2/4
Source:	Learned at 1954 Folk Festival staged by New York City Park Department.
Pattern:	Polka or Pas-de-Basque step. (The Russian version of the polka for

ballroom use is smooth with the feet kept close to the floor.)

MEASURES

Figure I Polka and Turn

1—2

2 forward polka steps starting on the outside feet (man's left, girl's right). On first pattern, inside hands swing forward and partners turn slightly away from each other. On second polka pattern, inside hands swing backward and partners face slightly toward each other.

3—4

Turning outward from partner make 1 complete turn with 4 walking steps (man to left, girl to right) while continuing to progress counterclockwise.

5—8

Repeat action of measure 1—4.

Figure II Balance Forward and Backward, Polka

9—10

In Varsouvienne position facing counterclockwise take 1 forward balance step (both starting on left foot), 1 backward balance step.

11—12

2 polka steps forward in counterclockwise direction.

13—16

Repeat action of measure 9—12. Finish facing partner with man's back to center of room.

Figure III Clap and Passing Polka

17—20

Clap own hands 2 times (count 1—2). Take 3 polka steps backward away from partner. (Man starts with hop on right, girl with hop on left.)

21—24

Clap own hands 2 times. Take 2 polka steps forward passing left to left shoulder with partner. Stamp 3 times (counts 1 and 2). Hold (count and).

17—20

Clap own hands 2 times. Take 3 polka steps backward passing partner's left shoulder. Finish close to and facing partner.

21—22

Clap own hands 2 times (count 1—2). Pause (count 1—2).

23—24

With 2 polka steps, make a complete circle away from partner. Man turns left, girl turns right.

NOTE: When the polka steps are taken in Figure III, the man crosses his arms at his chest. The girl places her hands on her hips.

GLOSSARY

Bleking step. 2/4 meter. Hop right extending left foot forward with heel touching floor (count 1 and). Hop left, extending right foot forward with heel touching floor (count 2 and). Hop right, extend left (count 1). Hop left, extend right (count and). Hop right, extend left (count 2). Hold (count and) or hop left, extend right (count and).

Buzz step swing. Step on right foot pivoting clockwise on the ball of the foot (count 1). The left foot in a short, direct line back of right foot pushes with the same action needed to move a scooter (count 2).

Clockwise. Indicates a direction moving with the hands of a clock. In a circle, it would be moving to the left.

Counterclockwise. Indicates a direction opposite to the hands of a clock. In a circle, it would be moving to the right.

Courtesy turn. A movement taken in place by a couple. Man's left hand joined with girl's left hand. Man's right arm around girl's waist. Man turns backward pivoting almost in place as girl moves forward counterclockwise. A full turn or a turn and a half is made.

Grand right and left. Partners face, join right hands, move forward passing right shoulders and join left hands with oncoming person. Moving forward passing left shoulders, join right hands with next person, and so forth. Men move counterclockwise around circle, girls move clockwise. In European dances, the word "chain" refers to a Grand Right and Left.

Grapevine step. Moving left, the right foot crosses in front of the left (count 1), step sideward left with left foot (count 2). Cross right foot in back of left foot (count 3), step sideward left with left foot (count 4). A grapevine step to the right starts with opposite footwork. This pattern also can be started with cross step in back.

Hey. An English term for a Grand Right and Left which is performed without joining hands. Dancers weave passing right and then left shoulders. A straight line *hey* is known in Scottish dances as a reel.

Line of direction. Indicates a counterclockwise direction.

Meter. The number of underlying beats in a measure of music. The top number of the meter states the number of beats existing in each measure.

113

The bottom number stipulates the type of note which receives the value of one beat. In 2/4 meter, the two at the top indicates two beats per measure and the four at the bottom stipulates that a quarter note receives the value of one beat.

Pas-de-basque.   Leap sideward (count 1). Step forward in front of supporting leg (count 2). Step in place or in closed position (count 3). In 2/4 meter, the steps are taken on the counts of 1 and 2, followed by a hold on the count of "and."

Push step.   Step sideward (count 1). Bring free foot to instep of supporting foot and push away forcing first foot to move sideward again (count and).

Quadrille.   A French term: *quadri* meaning four, and *drille* implying repetitive movements. Refers to dances designed for four couples in a square formation.

Reverse line of direction.   Moving in the opposite direction; in a circle, it would mean clockwise.

Sashay.   An American term. Dancers move around each other one time. Moving sideward right, man goes behind the girl. The girl moving sideward left goes in front of the man.

Step-arch.   Usually associated with the Waltz. Step sideward (count 1). Pull free foot to instep of supporting leg without weight (counts 2−3). In some dances, the sideward step receives the counts of 1−2 and the arch receives the count of 3.

Step-draw.   In 2/4 meter; step sideward (count 1). Drag free foot to closing position and transfer weight (count 2). In 3/4 meter, the free foot is dragged on the floor for the counts of 2−3.

BIBLIOGRAPHY

Folk Dance Federation of California, *Folk Dances from Near and Far, International Folk Dance Series*. Vol. A2 (1962), Vol. B1 (1959), Vol. C1 (1960). San Francisco, Calif.: Folk Dance Federation of California.
> Collections of dances reprinted from the Folk Dance Federation magazine, "Let's Dance." Vol. A2 contains beginning dances; Vol. B1 contains intermediate dances; Vol. C1 contains advanced dances.

Hall, Tillman J., *Dance!* Belmont, Calif.: Wadsworth Publishing Co., Inc., 1963.
> A guide to social, folk, and square dancing, with instructional material and dance descriptions suitable for beginning and intermediate dancers. Brief information given on soft shoe and tap dancing.

Haskell, Arnold, *The Wonderful World of Dance*. Garden City, N. Y.: Garden City Books, 1960.
> A brief history of the sources and development of dance. Excellent illustrations.

Lawson, Joan, *European Folk Dance, Its National and Musical Characteristics*. London, England: Sir Isaac Pitman and Sons, Ltd., 1953.
> A scholarly writing for persons interested in furthering their knowledge and understanding of European folk dancing.

Lidster, Miriam D., and Tamburini, Dorothy H., *Folk Dance Progressions*. Belmont, Calif.: Wadsworth Publishing Co., Inc., 1965.
> A source book of 120 international folk dances established according to pattern and graduating in difficulty from simple to complex. Background studies of the Philippine Islands, Israel, and the Balkan and Scandinavian countries are included.

Mann, Kathleen, *Peasant Costumes in Europe*. Combined Edition. New York: The Macmillan Co., 1950.
> Previously consisting of two volumes, this edition contains over 130 pages of drawings and some color plates, with a brief historical resume of each of the countries represented.

Mynatt, Constance V., and Kaiman, Bernard D., *Folk Dancing for Students and Teachers*. Dubuque, Iowa: Wm. C. Brown Company, Publishers, 1968.
> Contains instructional materials and dance descriptions representative of twenty nations. Suitable for persons first learning to folk dance.

Wakefield, Eleanor E., *Folk Dancing in America*. New York: J. Lowell Pratt and Company, 1966.
> Written primarily for teachers of folk dancing but contains a vast amount of material and dance descriptions of interest to beginning as well as advanced dancers.

PERIODICALS

Country Dancer, The Country Dance Society of America, 31 Union Square West, New York, N. Y. 10003. Published irregularly.

Let's Dance, Folk Dance Federation of California, Inc., 1604 Felton St., San Francisco, Calif. 94134. Published 10 copies per year.

Northern Junket, Ralph Page, Editor. 117 Washington Street, Keene, N. H. 03431. Published monthly.

Rosin the Bow, 115 Cliff Street, Paterson, N. J. 07522. Published quarterly.

Sets in Order, the Official Magazine of Square Dancing, 462 N. Robertson Blvd., Los Angeles, Calif. 90048. Published monthly.

Square Dance (formerly American Squares), Arvid Olson, Editor. 1622 N. Rand Road, Arlington Heights, Ill. 60004. Published monthly.

FOLK DANCE RECORD SUPPLIERS

It is suggested that local record dealers first be contacted since many of them stock folk and square dance records. Venders listed below supplying records other than their own are marked with an asterisk.

*Canadian Folk Dance Record Service, 605 King Street, West, Toronto, Ontario, Canada.

Educational Dance Recordings, Bridgeport, Conn. 06611.

*Festival Folkshop, 161 Turk Street, San Francisco, Calif. 94102.

*Folk Dance House, 108 West 16th Street, New York, N. Y. 10011.

*Folklore Imports, 4220 Ninth Ave. N.E., Seattle, Wash. 98105.

*Folkraft Record Co. (Dance Record Center), 1159 Broad Street, Newark, N. J. 07114.

Folkways Records and Service Corp., 117 West 46th Street, New York, N. Y. 10036.

Imperial Record Co., 137 N. Western Ave., Los Angeles, Calif. 90004.

Israel Music Foundation, 731 Broadway, New York, N. Y. 10003.

Kismet Record Co., 227 East 14th Street, New York, N. Y. 10003.

Olympic Record Company, 312 West 51st Street, New York, N. Y. 10019.

Radio Corporation of America (RCA), Victor Record Division, 155 East 24th Street, New York, N. Y. 10011.

*The Record Center, 1614 No. Pulaski Road, Chicago, Ill. 60639.

Windsor Record Co., 5528 N. Rosemead Blvd., Temple City, Calif.